CALLED
BY
THE
SPIRIT

For Such A Time As Now

The Inspirational Writing

of

Trevor C. Belmosa

Order this book online at www.trafford.com
or email orders@trafford.com

Most Trafford titles are also available at major online book retailers.

The views expressed in this work are solely those of the author and do not
necessarily reflect the views of the publisher, and the publisher hereby
disclaims any responsibility for them.

Printed in the United States of America.

ISBN: 978-1-4269-4088-0 (sc)

Library of Congress Control Number: 2010914174

*Our mission is to efficiently provide the world's finest, most comprehensive book publishing
service, enabling every author to experience success. To find out how to publish your book, your
way, and have it available worldwide, visit us online at www.trafford.com*

Trafford rev. 11/05/2010

Trafford PUBLISHING® www.trafford.com

North America & international
toll-free: 1 888 232 4444 (USA & Canada)
phone: 250 383 6864 • fax: 812 355 4082

To people who love Jesus Christ, to people who are led by the Holy Spirit, and to people who will come to know and accept Jesus as their Lord and Savior and to people who will thank God, the Father, for sending Jesus Christ as His visible image to us on earth to save us from sin and to give us an everlasting abundant life.

To my wife, Tracy, to Makeda, our daughter and to her generation, and to my sons, Nekoro and Omari, and to my dear mother, Lorna Belmosa, my sister, Marilyn, my brother, Victor and to all my relatives.

I pray that as you read this book it will encourage you to answer God's call to salvation and prosperity. I dedicate my experiences, thoughts and prayers in this book to the kingdom of God and may it be useful in bringing glory to His Name and to His Work among us.

Table of Contents

CHAPTER 1

PLANTED BY THE RIVER

"And he shall be like a tree planted by the rivers of water…" Psalm 1:3

King JamesVersion, Amplified Holy Bible, Zondervan, 1995

Aboard USS Mt. Vernon

Chapter 1 - Introduction: Waking Up

Planted by the River is a collection of writings which cover a 10-year period from 1976-1986. These writings reflect thoughts and experiences which captured moments when I became awakened to a deeper awareness of myself and the existence of a living God.

I attempted to describe what I identified as my spiritual 'rebirth' and 'planting' into the 'calling' of the 'things' of God.

I was 21 years old and on my 1st year of military duty in the U.S. Navy when I faced several personal and social challenges which forced me to retreat, to reassess my purpose for being in the military, my purpose for being alive on this earth and to rethink the goals I desired to achieve in the future.

The initial phase of my writings got started at the Naval Base in Coronado, San Diego, California where I was stationed. These writings were sparked by a combination of soul searching experiences which began immediately upon my return from a six- month tour of duty off the coast of Cambodia in 1975 where I had participated in the Cambodian Refugee evacuation exercise.

My 6 months tour of duty on the USS Mt. Vernon took us around the coast of the Pacific Ocean where we landed at various ports. The ship docked in such places as the Philippines, Hong Kong, Taiwan, Nagasaki and other regional areas which included Cambodia.

Upon my return from the pacific coast to home base in San Diego, California, I began to experience profound attitudinal changes in my relationship with my live-in girlfriend who was also in the navy. This led to a 'break up' and separation. My heart was broken. In addition to my emotional pain, many of my close friends who had returned from Cambodia with me were relocated to other military bases. The lost of these friendships were painful. Then, added to all that hurt, I was suddenly confronted with prejudicial attitudes and racist behavior from a few 'white' officers who attempted to block my High School transcript and application form which I had submitted for review and approval.

I had sought advancement and further education in order to upgrade my skills and prepare for the future, but they utilized a 'delaying' tactic by not attending to them in a timely fashion. They also rationalized their behavior by accusing me of not behaving in the stereotypical manner when ordered (even with obscene language) by fellow officers. They felt that I did not 'jump' in fear or that I didn't respond as a 'fully indoctrinated' sailor when commanded.

Despite their negative motivations, I did sought help from other 'white' officers who pushed forward my documents and encouraged me to stay the course. I was eventually accepted for further educational training.

However, with all of these challenges before me, I truly missed my immediate family: my mother, father, sister, brother, and my extended family that lived nearby in Queens, New York. I was young, lonely, heart - broken, wounded by others and so I went into a state of reflection and solitude. I visited the library on the naval base and I began to read books to search for answers to the problems that I faced.

I recalled being influenced by such books as: Identity and Intimacy by Kilpatrick; Modern Man in Search of Manhood by Greene; To Be A Slave by Lester; The Fire Next Time by James Baldwin; Where Do We Go From Here by Dr. Martin Luther King, Jr. and The Prophet by Khalil Gibran.

These books gave me insight on man's search to find himself, his search to understand the world around him, to understand his soul's purpose and the role of God in his life. These readings also made me aware of the history and struggles of American people of African descent, other racial and gender groups in America and the fight of people all around the world for a better life. I learned that people fought for freedom from all forms of oppression, exploitation and limitation.

Yet, there was still a yearning in my soul to understand why I was facing all these negative forces all at same time. I had never lived with a woman and then had to leave unexpectedly especially because I said that I wasn't ready for marriage. I had never lost close friends so quickly especially after we had looked out for each another in a combat zone. I had never experienced institutional racism before because I grew up in Trinidad, in the Caribbean where racism was not overt. Also, I was never on my own without family members living nearby as a support mechanism.

These life issues were new to me because previously I was having fun in the military especially after duty. It was all about "wine, women, drugs and party". But, now, I was torn, confused and faced with decisions about the state of my heart, my soul, my future and life around me.

In this state of contemplation, an African-American military friend, who was a Christian, told me that I should read the Bible because I would find answers to my situation. I said ok and he, then, loaned me his Bible.

Now, I was twenty-two years old, and to my recollection I had not read any pages of the Bible since I was about ten years old while attending a Catholic Boys School in Trinidad. All I remembered reading in school was the catechism and using the Holy Rosary to pray at the Roman Catholic Church in Port of Spain where our school took us and where I was confirmed. I recalled seeing the crucifixion of Jesus Christ inscribed on the walls of the Church and I was also interested in becoming an acolyte, but, I didn't pursue it any further because I felt confused after observing the priest counting the collection and sipping constantly on 'real' wine.

I also remembered my grandmother's church, a Spiritual Baptist Church which taught from the Bible, but which also included some African rituals of the Shango and Orisha beliefs. I knew that the preacher lived in the village among us and there was a lot of drumming and dancing and praising, and falling out during the services. I didn't understand any of this type of worship as a child. I just enjoyed the food and listened to the preaching without understanding any of it.

Nevertheless, that night, at the naval base, in my room, I began to read this black covered Bible. I was reading the words in the book of Psalms and Proverbs. I was amazed. I read through those books and scanned through the Gospel from night into the morning. I felt a change of attitude overcome me. I somehow had gained inspiration and courage to stand-up and to confront the negative forces and the problems which were pushing me into a mode of depression and isolation. I was so excited. I was full of life but in a different way, a more serious way. I believed it was a spiritual way similar to being like a soldier at war against evil. I became aware of another way of life, a godly way where I was filled with a spirit of strength and power from the words that I had read.

I returned my friends' Bible and I got hold of a small green colored New Testament Bible which I carried with me every day. I took every opportunity to read and to pray during any free moment I got as I worked on my military tasks. Suddenly, my mind was transformed from confusion to clarity by the words in Psalms and Proverbs. Anytime any negative feelings or words came up in me or at me, I just took solace in the words of the Bible and I felt comforted and revitalized.

I began to record my new found feelings and thoughts in a diary. I recalled once what a few of my military buddies said to me one day as we hung out. They exclaimed, "What happened to you? You don't drink anymore, smoke 'weed' anymore? Every time we visit your room to watch the game, it's like we're in Church. You're not cool anymore, man." I told them that it was Jesus; that something had happened to me when I read the Bible but they kept on looking at the football game and I joined them. We were still friends even though I had changed and only spoke about what the words of Jesus had done to me.

In fact, I want to share one of the writings I had recorded in my diary about the profound transformation I had gone through after being armed with the words of God in the Bible.

This is what I recorded in 1976:

"My attitude seems very different I seem to be unique
and that uniqueness is mainly because of the drink
I was given by my best friend. He shared with me
out of his cup of love a drink that transformed my whole life
… All the pain and changes are behind me now. My road seems
clear.
All obstacles so far have been overcome… Since I have seen the
light I want more and more of that love. For it has carried me for
quite a distance in the darkness. Now that I am aware of such
sweetness I am running like a long distance runner to it, for I
know love called me and answered me when I needed it. Love is
the way."

Although I felt that love had called me and answered me in my times of trouble, the spiritual thirst for more understanding led me to another fountain of wisdom which did not include Jesus Christ.

In discussion about God with a Jamaican military friend, he introduced me to a book titled: The Philosophy of the Masters, by Huzur Maharaj Sawan Singh Ji, Sant Satguru of the Radha Soami Satsang Beas, Punjab, India.

The teachings of these Masters on the Science of God-Realization practiced while living in this world captivated me and paved the way for my interest in finding God within. I was guided on the path of seeking oneness with God through meditation. Although I was deeply attracted to the teachings and the practice of meditation, I did not get initiated into the Satgurus' way of life. I was deeply touched by the essence of its message. This is what I recorded in my Diary in 1977 when I was engrossed with the teachings of the masters.

> **" You are the part that I lost when time and space came between us. Now that we have found each other after so many heartaches and pains of search... you are the light that makes life's purpose come true ... the tears in my eyes show that I am happy ... you have broken my seal. I love you ... you gave me wings to fly very high."**

This was the state of my mind at the time when I used meditation to seek God within myself. I had learned from Jesus that the Kingdom of God was within us and I was looking for a method to guide me to God. Meditation opened my spiritual awareness and broke a seal which led me to search even harder and deeper to find God because the Bible described Him as being near you and in you.

All this time that I was engaged in my search for God, I studied and practiced right living on my own. Rarely did I attend Church or met with any meditation group. I was in the military and I performed my duties and I lived for God based on my understanding and guidance from my inner voice. I didn't know Jesus but I accepted Him and He changed me, nor did I know the guru, but the meditation techniques taught me to focus within myself in order to find God.

And, I debated with myself as to if love was an It, a nameless entity, a universal force beyond me and was only attainable if you strive to merge your inner-self into oneness with the nameless it, or was love a vast expanse floating blissfully and aimlessly in the heavens and all I had to do was to use my mind to feel love from it and then accentuate the positive and ignore the negative. I felt that love was more than an It or a universal essence without manifestation. I felt that love was spiritual, that love had a personality outside of me and can manifest inside of me. As I came to know about God's words, especially about the gospel of Jesus Christ and the spirit and life of His words which manifested the spiritual power of love within me, I felt love was truth. It was truth that transformed my mind which was confused about life's issues. His truth set me free to face the challenges and not to be overwhelmed by them.

Yet, at that time of introspection, I operated with a sense of inner peace, a fullness of love and strength and a passion to know more about God. I wrote down a lot of my thoughts, feelings, and experiences on a daily basis.

In 1977, I had completed my educational credit requirement and I was transferred to Meridian, Mississippi to attend Military A School for Disbursing. While at Meridian, away from the city of San Diego, I spent a lot of time writing, meditating, observing nature and its beauty, praying and talking to God, and trying to find myself. I often asked God what was happening to me since I was not acting as the other young people in the military. I was a vegetarian, celibate, peaceful, focused, studious and obedient. I questioned my thoughts and actions but I was at peace with myself.

I completed my course with honors at Disbursing School and I was sent to Norfolk, Virginia to the USS Charleston.

Shortly, thereafter, the ship made a six month tour near the Mediterranean Sea where I visited places in Italy such as Naples, Venice, Sardinia, and we also ported in Barcelona, Spain.

Upon our return to Norfolk, I had completed my four years of military service. I was now a civilian and my future choices were ahead of me. In 1978, I left the naval services with an honorable discharge, a good conduct award medal, a national defense medal,disbursing and administrative skills, travel experience, an inner awareness of God, an awakened love for Jesus Christ and a 'knowing' that the words of the Bible are powerful tools of truth.

Immediately, after arriving and settling at home in Queens, New York, I enrolled at Medgar Evers College, in Brooklyn, New York to pursue a Bachelors' Degree. I was on a new path of seeking an education for employment in the society. But, the spiritual aroma of my previous lifestyle lingered on as a sweet smelling fragrance during my first few months of College. Then, in the 1980's, I became engrossed in the studies of history, psychology, science, statistics and government, and, internally, my belief system was becoming politicized and socialized. I mentally blended God with politics. I saw Jesus as a revolutionary who fought against the oppressors of His time. I saw Jesus' humanity and I wanted to be a leader of His caliber.

I got involved in the students' organizations on campus and I got engaged in protest actions at Medgar Evers College. I participated in community protests and marched against unjust national and international issues while in college. I also gave up on my vegetarian diet. I was no longer celibate and I engaged in 'casual' marijuana smoking and 'casual' alcohol drinking.

During my course of study, I travelled to Egypt to learn about ancient Egyptian civilization and the belief system of Osiris, Isis and Horus and the Pharaohs. I went into one of the pyramids and into one of the tombs in the Valley of the Kings. I visited the famous Temple of Luxor, the Cairo Museum, a Nubian village and other noted sites. I also examined the belief systems of monotheism and polytheism in Egypt.

I travelled to other nations such as Senegal where I visited an ancient mosque because I had a lot of questions on Islam and its impact on Africans and the modern world. I travelled to Ghana, Cuba, Grenada, Puerto Rico and Barbados. I studied capitalism, socialism, Marxism, the works of Lenin and Moa Zedong, Pan-Africanism, Indian and Arab Nationalism and the African-American leader Malcolm X and the Nation of Islam and Martin Luther King Jr. and the Civil Rights Movement, the Women Rights Struggle and the Hispanic peoples' and Native American struggles, and the struggles of immigrants to the shores of America, the Revolutionary War, the Civil War and the World Wars and Americanism.

During my college years, I got married and fathered two boys. I wrote profusely about topics related to politics, romance and spiritual life. In 1981, one of my written pieces won a college-wide poetry and prose competition. It was written about New York City and titled Modern City. This is what I wrote.

MODERN CITY

Civilization standing naked and still
Reaching for the unknown
beyond the minds of humankind
City of wealth, money and power
Greedy for control of the world
Civilization dying of a lack of
human growth
City empty of humanness
Lost in the flow of sin
Release your chains of material
illusions and set the people free
Civilization standing naked and still
There is still time for freedom
Open up your gates of love
and be like the mighty ocean of
human kindness
Be strong. Be just
Or face the wrath of destruction.

This was my thinking of modern technological life in New York City, and the symbolism of the World Trade Center with its over-towering reach upward to the sky and the awesome power it welded in world affairs at the time. That written piece represented an appeal for change and a warning of impending wrath if it was not heeded.

Finally, in 1983, I completed my Bachelors' program and immediately obtained employment as a community counselor and trainer of adult workers in a Brooklyn based Developmental Disabilities Program. In 1985, I enrolled in the Masters' Degree course at the New School for Social Research in Manhattan, New York and attended classes in the evening after work. I completed the Master's Program in Political and Social Science in 1987.

Throughout these 10 years of my life, the thirst for spiritual enlightenment was not quenched. The 'rebirth' or 'awakening' or "waking up" that took place in my life as a youth on the U.S. Naval base in San Diego had transformed my mind into in an avid seeker after truth, love, justice, and the need to fully answer an inner call which was then partially answered by the words in a Bible which I borrowed from a friend who saw that I needed help and this spiritual thirst grew and became mentally interwoven with my academic studies as I grew into a young adult.

As you read the poems, prose and comments in **Planted By The River,** visualize the awakening of a soul to an inner call by the voice of love whispering and beckoning it to drink from the fountain of water of the living God.

You Called Me

O Savior, You called me
day and night
and I turned away in fright

O Savior, Like the shadows
of my dream
You showed me the path
I have to travel

But, I ignored Your whisper,
Your inner voice
How long, My Savior,
Do I have
a Choice?

O Savior, I marvel at Your
enduring calls
This time, I will, be still,
And, be not afraid

I will obey and come to You
And, just do,
What You called me
To Do

Trevor C. Belmosa

Hidden Secret

Oh God, Shadows of Your light seem so dim
And my Soul is in need of Your love
Days and veils of darkness cover my mind
And I'm lost: a helping hand I cannot find.
Beautiful feelings and sweet dreams
are no longer near. Why! How could life
be so unfair?
Searching where I cannot take my mind,
I hope to find, Your Ocean of divine love
Because my heart tells me that I'm a drop
of a hidden secret which flows within and
above.
Oh Lord, Your presence, washes away all my
pain and sadness, and my soul rejoices with peace
and joy in Your radiance.
What a mystery for my mind to accept?
For, it is Your arm of righteousness and Your precepts
and glorious songs which kept me strong
and where I belong.
Yes God, Your love has healed the ugliness of life
and I now know that the message abiding in my Soul,
in due time, is Your hidden secret which will unfold.

Cloth of Love

I can feel the tears running
down my heart
For loneliness has become
my cloak
Love has left and my mind
 is troubled
Looking at life and at us
working, busy talking, living
and enjoying what we consider
'goodness' in this world
Yet, I feel there is more
to the things I see
How can I calm this confused
feeling inside of me?
I'm lost in a wonder
and I'm in need
of a cloth of love
to dry my bleeding heart
For the glitter of this world
brings darkness over my eyes, and
I cannot see the 'true' light
Come! Comforter, Help me remove
this cloak of loneliness and kindly
use Your cloth of love
to wipe my tears away.

Trevor C. Belmosa

A Spirit

There is a Spirit in me
Who can't rest
A Spirit that yearns
For liberty
A Spirit who sees the evils
of the world
And desires to spread
Freedom, love and security

The tears in my eyes
are the pain that I feel
Because this Spirit in me
Cannot rest in dignity
The injustice, the suffering and
the hate, they are the enemy to me
O God, help us…help me
Loose these chains of wickedness
binding us in captivity

Yes Lord, Free the Spirit
within me
So I can find peace and rest
in You, and You alone,
and not in what I see
For my Spirit desperately need
Your reality! Your eternity!

Climb The Mountain

To Love
Is to
Climb the mountain
Of despair
Just
To find
The water of tranquility
Running deeply
In your own
Heart.

Trevor C. Belmosa

My Guiding Light

May the blessing
of God
be upon me
to inspire me and
to lead me
in the way and path
 of righteousness,
justice, peace
and love

At this time
of deep conflict
and distorted thoughts
May the Lord make all things
visible and understandable

In these times
of frustration and loss
May God ease the confusion
and stress and let His Truth
be my guiding light.

Back To the Center

In the depths
of my being
I thank the Spirit
for renewing me,
for leading me
back to the center
of myself

O! What a wonderful
feeling of goodness,
kindness, meekness and
quietness

It is so good to be me
Again
To be one with the Spirit
of God
within me.

Trevor C. Belmosa

Am I?

In the morning when the joy of light
Awakens the world,
I wonder about love and Am I loving?

Like the cool breeze caressing every corner
of our daily travel,
I wonder about touching, holding and feeling
And, Am I reaching out?

In the stillness of the night when darkness
engulfs our sleeping moments,
I wonder about humility and Am I forgiving?

Like the Spirit of celebration and jubilation
forever embracing the smiles of our hearts,
I wonder about laughter, joy and peace, and,
Am I truly living righteous with my family,
friends and neighbors?

In the beauty of life where love kisses the truth
of our darkness and turns it into victory,
I wonder about myself, and, Am I loving
myself as God commands me to and Am I
loving God with all my heart, mind and strength?
Am I loving? Am I reaching out? Am I forgiving?
Am I living righteous? Am I loving myself? Am I
loving God? Am I? Am I, Holy Spirit?

Dance to No One's Blues

Dance to no one's blues
But open your heart and
make joy your music
Be like a song,
Sung from the depths
of your positive experiences
and dance to no one's blues

Live, like the peaceful flow of the rivers
And spread honey over the pains
of your life
Make your tears sweet as nectar…but,
Dance to no one's blues

Love like the Spirit of humility
give to the deserving
and free the righteous,
but dance to no one's blues

Dance to the rhythm of tomorrow
Dance to the yet born
Dance to the setting and rising of the Sun
but dance to no one's blues

Why? For they can't dance for you
when you come before the Lord
to explain how you overcame your blues
by not dancing in the sinner's shoes.

Trevor C. Belmosa

Peace

Peace like the angel of love
surrounds me
and I feel a sense of relaxation
I am going to enjoy this peace

Because of all the calamities
taking place in the world, daily,
receiving Peace is a miracle

Oh, miracle of peace!
You have brought 'true' joy,
stay forever and abide in me, always.

Raindrops

You are like raindrops
washing away all the ugliness
of my days and nights

May your blessing be a cup of love
that I can drink and fill
my empty soul

Oh, love…Oh water,
So real, so cool, so wet
caress my body and let my soul
rejoice

Oh, Peace, oh Joy, don't stop falling…
oh raindrops…your loving touch,
yes, your droplets,
they're more precious
than gold

Oh, raindrops, raindrops, just rain,
just pour all over me
and refresh my soul,
O, living waters
from heaven,
You turned my sadness into gladness
and I feel purified.

CHAPTER II

GOING IN AND COMING OUT

"I am the door. If anyone enters by Me, he will be saved, and will go in and out and find pasture"   John 10: 9

The Christian Life Bible, Porter L. Barrington 1985

Water Baptism in Trinidad

Chapter II - Introduction: Looking In

Going In and Coming Out represents a collection of writings which cover a 5-year period from 1987-1992. These writings reflect a time when I faced tremendous hardships but I was able to maintain my composure and develop a greater understanding of God's will operating in my daily affairs.

By 1987, I had relocated from New York City to the country of my birth, Trinidad and Tobago. I was married and had two sons. I was 33 years old and I had a Bachelors Degree in Public Administration and a Masters Degree in Political Science. I relocated because of a desire to make a contribution to my community and to my country even though I had been away for over 17 years.

During this 5 year period, I worked among the poor as a community organizer, was involved in local and national politics, had meaningful spiritual experiences, wrote and published two books, was unemployed for long periods and also became financially unstable. My self-esteem was low and my 'manhood' as a husband, father, provider and leader had reached a low point. I engaged in 'loose' living and enjoyed the night life. I was broken internally and I was forced to examine myself and my relationship with God. I thought that God was tempting me but in fact I was the one who had turned away from God and was relying on my achievements and the pleasures of my desires.

Consequently, when these harsh circumstances began to bombard me, I was redirected within my soul to humble myself and to once more learn to call and to depend on God for my strength and guidance.

In 1989, a defining moment came in the midst of my hardships, a female co-worker at SERVOL, a Catholic based Youth Training Program where I earned a low wage, introduced me to a Spiritual Baptist Church where she was a member. Co-incidentally, the Church she took me to was located in the same community where I was born and grew up until I was 15 years old before I flew to the Unites States to live. It is called John John, Laventille. It is one of the poorest communities in Trinidad.

However, in this church, most of the elders and members knew my deceased grandmother, my parents and some remembered me. One of my god-mothers was a member of this church. It is a Christian and Bible based church with traditional African influences which were added during the slavery era. There were no African ancestor worship, no other deity worship but God, the Father, the Son, Jesus Christ and the Holy Spirit. This faith is quite popular in Trinidad and Tobago.

Nevertheless, I recalled feeling as though God had orchestrated this move out of His infinite mercy when I was at my lowest point in my re-assimilation back home. He arranged for me to reconnect physically and spiritually with my birthplace and the place of worship where the people I had grew-up with as a child fellowshipped. They reached out to me and I felt accepted.

At this Church, I met Reverend Stephens, a very stern and disciplined spiritual teacher. Under his mentorship, I received 'water baptism' in the Caribbean Sea, and went through my first journey in the spirit which is called 'mourning.' It is a practice similar to the Daniel's fasting and praying on the ground of the earth as recorded in the Old Testament.

In preparation for this spiritual exercise which took place in a room with a dirt floor and a stone as one's pillow, I had to spend some time on 'mercy seat', a seat (a bench) where one sits for a period of time at church meetings as an indication of being purified from sinful, sexual or any form of conduct or thoughts which were not acceptable in readiness for isolation, deep meditation, fasting and prayer.

I entered this 'mourning' journey in the spirit for seven days and nights in that unlit room. While separated from the normal routine of life, I fought many inner negative forces, met many friendly forces, received a lot of information, developed strength in my inward parts, received a new heart from God and the depth of my spirit was connected to the depths of God's Spirit.

I successfully completed the 7 days of 'mourning'. It was truly a spiritual victory against evil forces within me. Pastor Stephens told me that I was led by God to prepare my soul and spirit through this form of denial because he saw that tough times were ahead of me. He was truly a visionary in God's vineyard.

As I mentioned earlier, I was a community activist involved in political and cultural activities. I was also an executive member and Commander of the American Legion Post 1992, the first American Legion in the English speaking Caribbean.

Then, suddenly, in 1990, the Red House, the seat of Political Power of one of the strongest Parliamentary Democracy and Republic in the Caribbean region, was violently attacked and briefly captured by armed Muslimeen, an African-Trinidadian Islamic Sect.

After several days of chaos and armed conflict, the local military and police forces regained control and the power was returned to the democratically elected politicians. A parliamentary representative, who represented the constituency where I resided, had died during the attempted coup. As a registered member of the then newly formed United National Congress political party, I was elected by that opposition party to run in a special bye-election for that vacated seat. I was the UNC's first political candidate in its first political electoral campaign. I had become a known 'political' personality but the party lost at the polls.

In 1991, the following year, I ran for office to represent the constituency where I was born but I lost again. Nevertheless, as a national executive party member, I was appointed to serve in the Senate for six months as an opposition Senator in the Parliament of Trinidad and Tobago. I was given the opportunity to make a brief contribution in the halls of Parliament on behalf of my home town and my country of birth. I had partially accomplished one of my goals for relocating to Trinidad in a relatively short period of time.

However as time passed, I became disenchanted with the two-fold nature of my lifestyle. I lived up to a public image while privately suffered financially and emotionally. I did not have a financial base and I was still 'green' to local and national politics. It was difficult to obtain employment as a political person especially being in one of the opposition parties as well as living in a small island nation where most people knew about you and are cautious about political hiring.

My family felt the strain and the pain of the loss of a main income earner. Consequently, in 1992, I resigned from the UNC political party and enlisted into the People's National Movement party which was also in the opposition but I never got actively involved with the PNM. I remained committed to helping the poor while I took a neutral position on party politics. However, the reality of joblessness impacted my lifestyle and I saw myself as a 'poor' popular political figure who struggled to stretch $5.00 into $55.00 dollars. I began to learn to do without a lot of things which I had taken for granted so I retreated from politics. I was not attending church during this time and I resorted to living a 'loose' life. I drank alcohol, womanized and smoked 'weed' discreetly. I never smoked cigarette because I didn't like the taste and the smell of my breath after I had one try. During this financial hardship, I instinctively returned to leaning on my own efforts and intelligence to get by in my daily affairs. I began to deeply understand the courage and the strength that poor people needed in order to survive from day to day. I did not live in poverty but the spirit of poverty was binding me because it was the first time in over eighteen working years that I felt broke. I did not have a job to wake up to go to and I did not have a salary to receive in order to contribute towards the bills, grocery, education and clothing of my sons nor had I any finances to assist my wife.

Many times I questioned myself. Why was I going through these difficult times? I had a Bachelors' and Masters' Degree, several Certificates, military training and many years of working experiences. Yet, all these qualifications could not stop the downward spiral I had to experience. My ego was bruised and my pride had collapsed. I once was popular but now I had nothing financially. I was tormented and puzzled. As I pondered on my lowly external state, I thought of my responsibility towards my wife and my sons. I saw that I had fallen into the negative cultural norms of manhood and didn't realize my selfishness nor recognized the error of my ways. I reflected on my initial goals for relocating to Trinidad and I questioned, 'What went wrong'? Then, in pain and without thinking, I began to pray instantly for guidance.

Then, as I returned to praying regularly and daily, I noticed a common trend emerging during the darkness of the times. God did not knock me down totally nor did any hurt came upon me physically or mentally. There was still an opportunity for me to get up and to start doing something positive every day. I began to look for the lesson to be learnt in everything that I did for the day. I prepared and planned an activity to execute on a daily basis. Moreover, I recalled the fast and prayer that I did in the Baptist Church and agreed with myself to practice fasting two to three days a week and to pray more and to read the Bible at nights before bedtime.

One night when I was reading the Bible, I found some scriptures which I had underlined about one or two years prior. These words just seemed to leap off the pages and jumped into my spirit and inspired and renewed my mind. These words were biblical verses from the Book of James. I recorded them in my diary because they were a unique inspiration. The words are as follows:

"… Humbly accept the words planted in you, which can save you." James 1:21
" Do not merely listen to the word, … Do what it says." James 1:22
" Perseverance must finish its work so that you may be mature and complete, not lacking anything" James 1:4
"Blessed is the man who perseveres under trial, he will receive the Crown of life that God has promised to those who love him." James 1:12

After being consoled by the Gospel of James that the difficulties I had been undergoing were truly God's way of disciplining me, since I had strayed away from depending on Him as my only source of love, peace, finances, success and hope, I had no other choice but to heed the further instructions of James' message.

"Submit yourselves, then, to God … Come near to God and He will come near to you. Wash your hands, … and purify your hearts, Grieve, mourn and wail … Humble yourselves before the Lord, and He will Lift you up." James 4:7-10

Inquiringly, I was thirsty to find out how to submit myself to God. So, I visited my uncle, Mr. Patrick Alfred, who lived on the Beetham Estate, another poor community in Trinidad. He was my spiritual mentor and biblical scholar, even though he was blind and did not earn a Ph.D. He knew the Bible, was a man of God and a good man. While exchanging spiritual ideas, I enquired about how can a person submit to God? He spoke about obedience, meditating on the Word of God, fasting and prayer, worship and service. He, then, presented me with a gift, one of his treasured books, The Aquarian Gospel of Jesus The Christ by Levi H. Dowling. He said it contained information about Jesus Christ which was not recorded in the Bible.

Interestingly, within the Aquarian Gospel, I found some insightful passages on how love and light can be obtained, that is, one of the ways that a person can relate to God. These particular passages stimulated my imagination. They stated:

"If man would find his savior, he must look within" pg.41
"God's meeting place with man is in the heart, and in a still
small voice He speaks: and he who hears is still" pg.65
"When man sees God as one with him, as Father- God,
he sees no middle man, no priest to intercede; he goes straight
up to him and says, My Father-God! And then he lays his hands
in God's own hand, and all is well." pg.65

This chapter also described one method that a person can practice in order to submit oneself to God. It explained about a 'Silence' where the Soul meets its God, but which cannot be seen by human eyes. The process of reaching this 'Silence' was stated like this.

"... When life's heavy load is pressing hard, it is far better to go
out and seek a quiet place to pray and meditate, ... When in the
Silence, phantom forms may flit before the mind; but they are
all subservient to the will; the master soul may speak and they
are gone,... Your human will must be absorbed by the divine;
then you will come into a consciousness of holiness. You are
within the Holy Place... all who enter are immersed in light,
and filled with wisdom, love and power." pg.79

The wealth of knowledge that I found in this book further confirmed some of the teachings and spiritual experiences which I had obtained in the past. Yet, it was a timely gift because the difficulties and the lean times that I faced in 1992 had forced me to do some soul searching. So, I found a quiet place at home when everyone left for school and work and meditated on Jesus' words in the Bible and submitted myself to God. I sought refuge in the Lord within and He created a peace within me and gave me comfort amidst the pain of life. I saw the beauty of His creation anew and He kindled a desire to enjoy life with the limited time that I had on earth. I realized that there was still a lot to learn about God's ways, and what I had to do for Him, and I had a lot to learn about how to depend on Him totally.

As you read the poems, prose and comments in **Going In and Coming Out**, open your soul to travel on a spiritual journey with me as I searched the depths of my inner chamber to seek God's face in order to renew my relationship with Him and to receive His instructions as to how to continue to walk in His ways while dealing with the outside world which bombarded our mind with cultural teachings which most people, including myself, followed blindly and fell into a cyclical pattern of terror and error; and, come see, with the aid of the inner teachings of truth by the Spirit of God, how the truth frees us from cultural bondage and releases us into the abundant life offered by words of Jesus Christ.

Trevor C. Belmosa

A Sweet Breath of Love

Love is a sweetness
that lingers in the heart
of the mind
And one can imagine
this sweetness over and over
again no matter what one is doing
or thinking about

Love is like an unforgotten kiss,
a sweet breath through
one's nostrils

Love is like a fragrance
whose aroma never fades

Love is the beauty of creation
born of a sweet eternal breath
from a loving God.

Ever Grateful

Lord, God, You know my needs
I ask only for Your grace and favor
My payments for labor is not great
It is not able to push me into a better
standard of living
But, God, who am I to be ungrateful
for the present wage.

You, Lord, know what I require for existence
but I am ever grateful for your sustenance
May I praise Your Name
For the small reward is better than none
And being able to provide some food,
clothing and shelter for myself and family
carry more weight in gold than the nakedness
of poverty that surrounds me.

Lord, God, I know Your blessings are many
and they come when You deem them, in Your season
and Your time
I wait patiently to improve my life
through hard work and Your loving mercy.

Lord, I am ever grateful that You are
the source of my life even in these tough times.
I will praise Your Name, as I go through the hardships
I will not complain. I will cry out to You but I will still be
grateful and thankful for being alive to hope and to have faith
for a better tomorrow.

Trevor C. Belmosa

God's Hands

I will put my hands
in God's hands and not worry about what
to do
I will take one day at a time because
something must come my way
which will bring an opportunity
for me to do what has to be done
in order to keep me active
and moving ahead in life
God knows I must follow
I'll be patient on the Lord
because my life, my success, and my future
is in God's Hands
And I know God's Hands
will never let go
of mine
I trust the hands of God because
His hands took the nails
for me

Your Grace and Mercy

Though I stand in the shadows
of Your greatness
I can feel the blessings of Your
grace and mercy

My life may not be in the best
condition or in the state I desire
but I have no fear

Everything in my life is as calm
as the wind that blows and soothes
the heat of the sun

For so great is Your love for me
that I ask only that Your
Grace and Mercy be with me
Until I see You in Your glory

Trevor C. Belmosa

I Stand By You

Lord, God, I wonder about Your mercy
Because even though things seem calm
and smooth I am not happy. I still have
an empty feeling about my life
God, why aren't I shouting for joy?
What do You think I should do?

O Lord, God, I stand by You
I seek Your guidance
What is it about my life that even though
no great suffering exist I am sad within my soul?

Is it Your Salvation and Holy Spirit I need?
If so, please, Deliver me! Save me! Empower
me! That I may serve You and stand by You
with joy in my heart and with peace in my soul.

O mercy of God, cover me,
As I stand steadfastly with my Lord
through the ups and downs, through
the trials and temptations, of this life.

O Lord, Now, that I know that Your mercy
is with me at all times I feel loved
My standing by You is not in vain.

Going Before The Lord

Today I prepared my soul to travel to meet
The Lord
Fasting and praying, enjoying the last moments
of normal life with my family and friends

I feel strange…desiring to be clean and pure,
and alone…yet not wanting to deny my feelings
to interact with others

Preparing to meet the Lord isn't easy, unsure of
what to do. Am I praying too much? What will
happen? Will I be safe? Am I ready?

O God, I just want to leave everything in Your hands
I don't know what I really want…I want nothing but
To see You, God and to let You fulfill Your Will
through me

Going to God isn't easy…preparing to meet the Lord
spiritually isn't easy…but I must go… into silence, go
in while praying and fasting
It isn't easy letting go of the worldly cares and the things
that we like
But, I must let go and travel within to seek His face…in
the Spirit

O Body, O Mind, O Will, Take your rest…Be still…I'm
going in, I'm going … before the presence of the Lord.

Trevor C. Belmosa

A Teacher's Wisdom

As you travel within to seek the Lord,
this is the time you have to pray like you
never prayed before
You must ask God to behold your true self
in order to find out who you are

Find out, What nation you belong to!
What work you have to do on earth!
Seek your spiritual name and number!

Always pray to God ... to Jesus Christ
Use your prayer keys constantly
You will travel spiritually and you will
See things, be not afraid ...ask a question,
Who are you? Where is this place? What is
here for me to obtain or to learn? Who can I talk to?

If you see a leaf, a stone, a branch, a person or
An animal ... Ask a question! Use your keys to
the kingdom because if you cease to pray then
you cease to fight! And, you will allow evil
forces to enter and distract or defeat you

This is a time for hard work, not sleeping or dreaming
But of humbling yourself before God, of asking God
to reveal what he has in store for you ... to solve your
problems to direct your destiny according to His plan

The body will feel pain. The mind will want you to quit
But prayers will remove all the fears, Prayers will remove
The darkest cloud

So, Just pray and pray and fast and talk to God in Spirit
and in Truth
It is the only way ... to meet Him ... and to receive your
Instructions
Heed these words ... so said, my Teacher.

Going In

I was lifted from mercy seat
for the time of washing ... of
my face, hands, arms and feet ...
had come
My head was anointed with oil
and I was given seven sips of water
from a cup

Now, it was time to pass from my
earthly routine to take up the task
of walking on the hard and narrow road
to communicate with my God in Spirit and
in Truth

Kneeling on the marked spot I was sealed
from head to feet with the breath of God's word
from the Bible then my head and eyes were
covered with swaddling cloth

Once I could have seen but now I was blind
My physical eyes were covered and I was now
to use my spiritual eyes on this journey
Then, after praise and worship, I was suddenly
spun around by the elders and with my face
downwards I found myself lying on the ground
entering the world of lights within myself

I began going in ... on the journey led by my spirit
... towards the kingdom of God, within.

Trevor C. Belmosa

The Inner Chamber

In the prison of the self, there I stood gazing
at darkness and lights
and at the silence of the self away from the
world of everyday activities

The pain of denial of food, sex, music, friends,
family and work … no bathing, no bed to sleep
on … this battle of letting go of life … in order
to gain sight of a greater life … ensued within me

Then, I realized, the slower I took to let go of the
worldly thoughts, the harder was my inner journey,
the heavier my task and the less time I had to communicate
with the Holy Spirit

Really this road was not easy to walk. I had to remain in
constant meditation, prayer and fasting
There were moments when I was lifted off the ground
and was given opportunities to share some of the visions
I had seen with spiritual co-workers who ministered to me,
who came from time to time to console and support me
with praises, songs, worship and prayer and even with sips
of warm water as the days and nights passed away slowly

O, this journey, in the inner temple, where I battled with the
inner forces, was no bed of roses
For many trials and temptations took place in this prism
of the self

I had to conquer my carnal desires in order to gain spiritual
understanding and wisdom from the Holy Spirit. The true
depth of myself had to surrender to the awesome depth of God

I soon recognized that all the blessings of the Lord resided in
the inner Chamber and I had to sacrifice and discipline myself through
this journey in order for peace to be victorious over my body, my flesh
and my mind.

God is the master in the inner chamber. There is no personhood there
only Spirit.
Then, the Spirit of God took charge of my inner nature and operated
on my heart.
My life was placed on a scale and weighed then a new me stood up
sealed with a vision, that only He has the key to release at the appointed
time.

God is Lord in the inner chamber and my spirit was set free
to worship Him before His glory. I rejoiced and celebrated in His
presence.
I was overjoyed to be in the inner chamber of God.
I had won this great victory over the negative inner forces of the world
within me,
with the aid of His Holy Spirit.

Trevor C. Belmosa

A Butterfly Appeared

On the last day of my journey in the spirit, after facing
great trials and tribulations, and after warring against the
evil forces of the inner and outer self
And, when I had completed praying and fasting for seven
days and nights seeking the face of God, here, I sat on
a bench called the seat of sorrow and sadness because the
moments were drawing near for me to return to the activities
of the world
As I sat, filled with the Spirit of the Lord and His anointing,
Praising and giving Him glory and honor silently, inwardly,
and thanking Him for guiding me through it all
Suddenly, the cloth that covered my eyes came loose and as I
took a peek upwards, the first thing my eyes saw was a pretty
colored butterfly on the ceiling flapping its wings
I felt so glad and amazed to see such a visitor. My heart was
overjoyed … deep in my soul I felt as though there was a
communion with this butterfly … its presence was refreshing and
fascinating
Then, the elders came and unwrapped the cloth from my head and
eyes and released me to go forth from the inner chamber
When I stood up and looked for this beautiful butterfly, it was
gone, the visitation was over. I, too, had to leave and face the reality
 of living in the world.

Coming Out

Oh! How wonderful to see
the morning light
and to feel the fresh morning breeze
To see the dew drops on the leaves
and the lush green mountains

Ah! Yes! The beauty of life's
handiwork stares me with a newness
… a renewed joy of living

Oh, it is so wonderful to see life
with a spiritual understanding, to know
the true beauty and to appreciate its
importance and my limited time to
learn from it … to enjoy it… to be
grateful for my presence in it

Because, I now know, there is a fine
line between Earth and Heaven … Life
and eternal life … the physical and the
spiritual

Coming out from my journey within and
having to live and rely on things outside
of myself made it clear to me that it is the
Lord who created this beautiful world for us,
So that, we should love one another, live in peace
with each other, and prosper together

But, ah, I'm out again. And I need to take
One step at a time in this reality because I
just came out of the inner chamber of God.

Trevor C. Belmosa

Help Me Walk on The Road

I had fasted and prayed for seven days and nights
I ate no food but drank some warm water
I worked hard spiritually fighting negative forces
within me
I travelled in the Spirit to various places and spoke
to many people and saw many things and experienced
personal transformation
I stayed awoke late many nights in prayer even though
I fell asleep sometimes
Yet, I was happy in the manner in which I gave up the
daily attachments of life and concentrated on the task
of walking on the hard and difficult road of giving up
my soul before the altar of the Lord in order to get in
touch with my spirit and to connect with the Spirit of
God
When in His presence, I asked not for money or luxury
but for Him to greet my spirit and to allow me to receive
His will for my life and to help me walk on the road of
Righteousness, to believe firmly in Jesus Christ, His
Son, who saved me and told me that the kingdom of God
is within, and to allow the Holy Spirit to guide me on my walk
on the slippery road of life's ups and downs. The slippery road
of walking by sight, seeing the cars, the technology of the times,
relying on the job, caring about the emotional and physical
interaction of people and also having to walk by faith and in the
spiritual wisdom and benefits of God.
Ah, but walk I must, yet, with the secret of the ages, that the love of
God, the truth of Jesus Christ, and the power of the Holy Spirit
lives within me,
And, that my obedience to His love, truth and power is what matters
most,
For then He will manifest through me and walk with me.

God So Wonderful

O God I'm happy to know
that You are close to me

It is so wonderful to know
that You keep me close
to Your path

Strengthen me O Lord
Let me live always in Your
Wisdom, Knowledge and Understanding

Yes, God, how powerful and great and
Awesome You are
Yet, You considered me, You loved me,
You drew me out of the gutter of immorality
and wickedness
and You took me in, You did not reject me

God, You are so wonderful.

Trevor C. Belmosa

How Rich I Am?

When I look at my life, it seems tranquil, stable
and easy going
Yet, I do not have the luxurious things to
brag about
But, I feel so happy, so glad, so full of love

O God, I know it is You. It is because of You
in my life
You hold me up. You clear my path. You direct
my thoughts. You fill my cup with Your mercy
and grace

O God, how rich I am? So rich that I can shout
with peace in my heart and sing a sweet melody

Lord, I'm so glad Your will is my will.
My life is Your life.
Thank You, O Loving Father!
I'm Rich because of You. Wow! How rich I am?

Want God In My Life

I always say a praise to God many times a day
silently in my mind
sometimes I kneel with the Holy Bible and read
scriptures, psalms or teachings of Jesus Christ
quietly and listen to the inner voice

Many times I will close my eyes and talk to God
from my heart loudly and silently too. I relate and
communicate with God on a daily basis

When I lay in bed at night, I talk to God.
When I am walking, driving or travelling by
bus or train or in an airplane, I praise God

When I visit family, friends, co-workers, workplaces,
Or any institution or company, I whisper praises to
God and ask Him to protect me, to shower me with His
favor and to bless everyone around

Before I do anything, I acknowledge God, but I am
Ever mindful that God knows all before it is done
Despite that, I praise God for who He is, and for what
He does for me daily and for the days to come. I love to
share every detail of my everyday affairs with my Lord.
That's why I want God in my life, always. I worship Him.

CHAPTER III

BUILT UP FOREVER

"Rooted and built up in Him and established in the faith…"   Colossians 2:7

King James Version, Amplified Holy Bible, Zondervan, 1995

Book Launch at Medgar Evers College

Chapter III - Introduction: Holding On

Built up Forever is a collection of writings which were recorded during the period from 1993 to 1995. This work represents my confidence in the rejuvenating power and renewing Spirit of the Lord.

In the previous years until now, I had been unemployed for nearly 2 years. But, I found legal creative ways to assist in paying bills, feeding, clothing and sheltering my family. My wife worked and there was always great support and understanding from my family and friends despite the emotional, psychological and financial hardships.

Notwithstanding the challenges, I had developed an inner strength and patience which kept me balanced. I refused to be shaken by negative forces. I prayed, meditated and tried to live every day conscious of God's plan unfolding in everything I did.

My mental and spiritual balance was also kept through occasional church attendance, my reading of the Bible and other spiritually oriented books such as the Qur'an, Bhagavad-Gita, the teachings of Buddha, the I Ching, the Egyptian Book of the Dead, and many other self help and spiritual growth disciplines.

Then, in 1993, a friend invited me to participate in a course called "The Art of Living." It was an approach to life developed by Pundit Sri Sri Ravi Shankar, a renowned Spiritual Master in the Vedic tradition from Bangalore, India. This eastern approach included a method that entailed a breathing exercise, meditation, simple yoga and basic principles of daily living based on love and release which were all summed up in a concept called Right Vision and Purifying Action. Thereafter, I met Pundit Ravi Shankar. It was a fulfilling and peak experience meeting and talking with him privately. The course did provide me with a sense of relaxation, calmness, a renewing of vital energies and a new breath of life.

As my relationship with God became more intense, I felt God's grace operating in my life again because somehow I would be at the right place at the right time to receive something or to meet someone who would help me accomplish a particular task or I would earn some money for helping others.

Also, during this period, I interacted with several spiritual teachers from India, Africa and the Caribbean but I did not commit myself to any of these religious beliefs instead God armed me with the Bible as my source of illumination and the 'Word of God' as my measuring tool. I never wavered from believing in Jesus Christ even though I was not planted in any church nor had any formal teachings about Jesus. I was just being guided to hold on to Him. He was in my soul.

But, I did question myself as to why was I meeting so many spiritual teachers from these varied belief systems. I was led to Proverbs 15:22 in the Bible. It states, **"Without counsel purposes are disappointed but in the multitude of counselors they are established"** I felt comforted that my spiritual path had been proven. I had a revelation that God's power was flowing in my heart and that I was being molded for some unseen futuristic purpose of God. I did admit that I was not near perfect and that I had many more painful and joyful lessons to learn. However, I was confident that whatever I had to go through this time I would put God first because I realized that I couldn't get away from Him. And, he showed me the reason why that night when I read the Bible. He led me to Psalm 139, a psalm of David. It explained.

"Where can I go from Your Spirit?
Or where can I flee from your presence? V.7

"You know my sitting down and my rising up; ..." V. 2

"If I ascend into heaven, You are there: If I make
my bed in hell, behold, You are there." V. 8

"Even there Your hand shall lead me, And Your

right hand shall hold me." V. 10

"You have hedged me behind and before;..." V.5

The unique arrangement of these verses encouraged me and cemented a signpost in my spiritual relationship with God. I felt that He was watching out for me. He wanted to make sure that I stayed on track with His call on my life.

Suddenly in 1995, I was contacted for an interview by someone in the Human Resources Department of a quasi-government ran Youth Training Program because she saw the quality of work I did among disenfranchised youths. I was hired immediately as a Manager and 6 months later, I was promoted to Regional Administrator, and within a year, I was appointed to Regional Manager over national projects.

God had blessed me with prosperity, increase and growth in every area of my life. I was grateful to God. My income was above average and I was exceedingly happy for this ray of hope that beamed through the cloud of my financial despair which once hovered over my life. My manhood was strengthened as I walked in Christ mindedness, as I became built up in my intimacy with God.

As you read the poems, prose and comments in **Built Up Forever,** examine with me the beginning of the 'grounding' of my faith in the Word of God, and my heart-filled praise and gratitude for His blessings and the confidence He built up in me as a God who cares and who will provide when you keep your mind and heart on Him and walk in His ways.

Trevor C. Belmosa

God Is Life

God is a loving God because He cares
for you and for me daily

God is merciful because He allows
us to fulfill His will

God is powerful because He controls
us from birth to death

God is love because He understands
our pain and suffering

God is everything because He is in
Heaven and He is with us on Earth
at the same time.

God knows everything because He made
us to think of Him

God determines all things because He made
us to act on His behalf

God is the master of love because He gives
and takes away the hurts as we travel on life's
pathway

God rules because He told us that without Him
we are nothing

God directs because He pushes us in the way
we have to go

God builds and God destroys because He is
The Judge of Life yet we kneel and pray for long
life but He opens the Book of Life to say
"Yes" or No", "Right or Left", "Heaven or Hell"

God is the source of all life because it was by
His breath we came alive and have our being

God is the author and finisher of our existence
Because He is Spirit and He is life. He gives birth
To us and He receives us at the end of our life.

Trevor C. Belmosa

God Is Alive Within

The peace that I feel is from knowing
that God dwells within
It is knowing that God directs everything
I allow God to tell me how to respond to issues
How wonderful it is to know that God
is operating in my life?
How peaceful I am knowing that God is
there all the time?

Knowing that God is alive within
does not shelter me from the ups and
downs, the frustration and pain of living
But it does allow me the patience, the wisdom
and the understanding to not get deterred into
negativity or pity rather He helps me to
recognize how much I need Him daily to work
out my problems, to conquer my fears, and to
learn to love myself and to reach out to others

I praise God constantly for the dosage of peace
He releases within me in serious times of need
How good it is to know God lives within?
I'm only moved when He moves in me
Thank You God for being in me. You make
me come alive within.

Art of Living

The Art of Living is accepting the negatives
and positives of daily existence and moving
on to the next negative and positive experiences
that are to come

The Art of Living is not to hold on for too long
to any experience but to have faith in the present

The Art of Living is being aware of the natural flow
or rhythm of the moment and being prepared and
willing to confront whatever the realities of life
bring to your doorstep with the confidence that
there is nothing too difficult that cannot be solved

The Art of Living is celebrating the good and releasing
the bad and coming to the knowledge that you must
surrender all things into the hands of God and be led
by His Spirit

The Art of Living is living daily in His presence
in good and bad times
You should invite Him into your life. He will teach
you the art of living.

Trevor C. Belmosa

Communicate, Now

Without communication and understanding
how are you going to have love?
Love does not just get up in the morning
It just does not happen that way

Communicate with yourself, with your friends,
Your family, loved ones and with God
And you will see love dancing and singing
with laughter within your heart and soul

When you communicate, you break down
the barriers of isolation, fear and hatred
and you open up the windows of understanding
You build a bridge for love to come across and
greet you with a smile of happiness

Communicate and you'll get a response
Love will caress your message and create an
atmosphere of hope and understanding in the midst
of uncertainty and bitterness

Don't wait too long! Communicate, Now! Quickly,
and let healing, peace and love prevail over division,
separation or destruction.

Wisdom has a voice which leads to joy, hurry,
Communicate! And, bring goodness into your life.

What To Do?

Lord, What to do?
Just wait on the Lord!
All fight is worthless
Only the fight of patience
Will be most effective

So, aim your arrows
at your innermost self
and control the yearning
and expectation of wanting
all answers … right now!

This is what you have to do.

Just wait, wait … on the Lord
Time is in the hands of God
And your blessings
Will come, in God's time

So wait! Wait on the Lord!
This is what you must do.
This is what He wants you
To do.

Trevor C. Belmosa

Listen To The Voice

God is wonderful
He knows your future
He guides you
All you have to do
Is listen to the voice
that talks to you

Listen to the words
Of common sense echoing
within yourself
and just act on the advice
from God being
whispered within your heart

You just have to do good
and live righteous
Everything will fall into place
right before your eyes
at the right time

Just listen to His voice
And act on His words!
For God is good. He does things
to you today in order
for your future
to be in accordance with His will

God is beautiful and faithful
He won't let you down
Just trust in His goodness
And listen to the voice

He'll always tell you something
You need to know or you need to do

Remember! Listen to the voice
In your heart
and act on His words.

Open My Heart

O Love, You are just the one for me
when I need to open my heart
when my soul needs to whisper
its innermost secrets

O Love, when You are near
my body aches with desire
You light the torch
of my passion
and You make me
become a raging fire
for Your love

O Love, bring Your wisdom, bring
Your glory
let's rejoice to together
in unity and victory

O Love, You better let the spiritual
joy flow freely through the door
Of my soul

O Love, You are the one
I want to be with
when I need to share,
when I need to open ... my heart.

Hold On To The Lord

Do as God says
and walk in His footsteps
do not be shaken when
everything seems hopeless,
when no smile seems to come
on your face
when you don't want to wake up
to another day of emptiness, of no
laughter, of no money, of no new clothes,
no comfortable home, no good meal,
no job, no family, no friends or no love ones

Don't give in! Don't quit! Hold on to the Lord!
Yes, Pray! Pray from the depths of your suffering!
Pray with tears in your heart, Cry out to God,
And, do as God directs
Don't give up! Don't turn your back on life, and
Don't blame yourself or anyone else … Just Pray!
Hold on to the Lord and expect something good
To happen … Open your eyes and your heart
And let the Lord lead you

Just hold on, No matter how hard, how painful,
how sad, how sick, you are … you still can make it.
Do not sit or lay idle, doing nothing. Do not waste time
being negative or depress. Do something everyday!
Go out, reach out to others, Ask for help, and always
pray and do as God says. He will change the situation

God will talk to you, just take time to listen
don't let yourself talk to you, but you must talk to yourself
about overcoming, try to put the suffering and confusion out
of your mind
and spend quiet time with yourself and reason with God

Then, Walk, in God's footsteps and you will find peace and love
He will help you through it all. Just hold on to the Lord and He
will lift you up, and make everything better.
Just, Hold on to the Lord! And, you will see
how much He loves you.
Yes, You can hold on! You can do it, He'll help you, just try, Hold on to
the Lord and He'll take you to a better place, trust Him!

God's Grace

I am living by the Grace of God
He keeps me strong all day long
He is my leader and my teacher
I follow wherever he leads me
I know God is taking care of my life
It is all in His hands, all Glory to God
Because in bad times I can still wake up
to another day and find something to keep
me going, and, as long as I am able to be
active I know God's Grace is abundant
in my life
His Grace is keeping me alive. His Grace
is lifting me up over my troubles
What else could it be? It is by His Grace
I'm breathing the oxygen of life.

Trevor C. Belmosa

Love The Lord

I love the Lord even though my life
is not all well materially

I love the Lord even though I struggle
daily to hold on to the little I have
to live with

I love the Lord because I know He is
testing me with the difficulties I face
everyday … no work, no pleasures, no
'expensive' things

I love the Lord because I haven't fallen
flat on my face … yet
and He knows I am restless and anxious
to earn income with the talent, time and
skills that I possess

I love the Lord because in all uncertainties
and lack of opportunities I can still laugh,
smile and share a joke

I love the Lord because I know He is
Strengthening my character as I go through
the denial of certain comfortable habits of live

I love the Lord because I have hope
and I know His salvation and joy will overcome
me soon by His grace and mercy

I love the Lord because I cannot wait for that day
When He releases me to get finances, to purchase
'exquisite' things, to advance in the world and to allow
my spirit, soul and body to manifest harmony, happiness
and satisfaction

I love the Lord because at the end of all the these trials
I will be stronger and better able to confront
and overcome greater challenges to come

I love the Lord during these tough times
because He taught me to be calm under pressure
and to be peaceful during a crisis
that's why I'll never give up on Him even when
He blesses me. I will serve Him and worship Him

I love the Lord because He loves me more than I will
ever know. I just know it. That's why, I love the Lord.

Trevor C. Belmosa

Prayer and Faith

God is good
His mercy and
justice is long
on love
but impatient
against wrong doing

Prayer and faith
Are like twins
one strengthens the will
of the heart
And
the other fortifies
the Spirit
of action

Always let the
goodness
in your heart
be in one accord
with the righteous
thoughts in your head
that they can manifest
power in the things you do

Develop a prayer relationship
with God and let Him fill your life
with faith and actions
that speaks of love.

Do The Work

The heart is magnified by good actions
intended to benefit the Will of God

Just do the work and stand firm
God will lead the way through His Words
that will flow through you

God's interest is for you to live happy
while in His service to the needy

Just do the work and stand firm
and see His might and His power prevail
in the lives of those who come to know
Him and to those who serve His will

Just do the work with passion and reap
the greatest benefit of a lifetime, an abundant
life, now, and a jeweled crown on your head for
eternity.

Trevor C. Belmosa

God's Happiness

God's blessing of happiness
may not be material wealth
even though it could be access to riches

His happiness is the inner peace
amidst terrible pain and loss,
a calmness amidst calamity and destruction

God's happiness is the love of Him
in your heart regardless of the suffering you face

Having love for God in your heart
will keep you happy all the days
of your life whether you are prosperous
or you are in poverty

God's blessing of happiness is beyond
our circumstances yet it is the answer to all
our problems

When we desperately desire true happiness
All we have to do is ask Him and God will
give us the desire of our heart willingly.

Everlasting Existence

Oh, it feels so good to caress God's wings
And to mingle my emotions with God's soft
and tender heart beat

It is so sweet to savor the nectar of God's
beauty and splendor

Yes, it is so delightful to embrace the warm
and loving soul of God's everlasting omnipresence

My understanding cannot explain and my words cannot
express my heart's joy when I entered into the outstretched
arms of God's sustaining power and walked into His majestic
mansion beyond infinity

He's alive! He's real! Ah, His presence. It's the glory of God.

Trevor C. Belmosa

When I Need You

When I need You, I take time to be with myself,
to close my eyes and pray, to call Your name
until I feel the vibration of Your breath taking
me higher, within, nearer to You, Lord

When I need You, I visit the congregation of Your
people, and I allow Your gathered tongues in songs
and sermons to bring peace to my mind

When I need You, I visit the poor and needy, and,
when I listen to their afflictions, I become humble
but courageous and I am inspired to call on You to
to do battle against injustice and evil strongholds in
their lives

When I need You, I mingle with the rich and well-to-do
and when I hear their heart's cry, I am reminded to judge
fairly for I realized that I must overcome all prejudices
and pray for Your love and presence to heal their inner
wounds

When I need You, I work hard in Your service so that I
will be free of idleness and I will make time to always
praise and worship You and call upon You, because,
I will always need You just as the world needs You.

Thank You God

I feel so good today that I praise Your loving name
O Lord, You are truly the redeemer and giver of
salvation, the nectar and the honey that are poured
over the thorns and pains

There were days when I questioningly accepted the
harsh conditions that I faced

there were times that I silently pleaded about the little
wages and sometimes no wages that I received or did
not receive

There were times that I felt the trials and tribulations
were too many to carry
but through all those trying and challenging times, I
called on You, God, and You gave me the inner strength
to remain active, to think positive, and to wait, to wait
on You … O Lord

So, today and everyday, I thank You, God, for the wages
I receive now, I cannot complain
For the light that I see now, is filled with the brilliance
of untold possibilities
And, the patience that I have now, is due to the peace
that You, Lord, have built-up within me

I thank You, God, for I know now that I am no longer
a hidden secret because no matter what I do in life
Your guiding hands will point the way

And, Your grace and mercy will forever resurrect and renew
me and keep me looking stable in the eye-sight of the world
I thank You, God, because I know You and I are one … For
You have placed Your love in my heart to share with others

Trevor C. Belmosa

God, You are all that I have and will ever need to make it in
this world
Thank You, for blessing me so richly within and without, thank
You for being there for me. God, You, deserve countless thanks
that I cannot measure but that I can start in my heart and with my
lips. "Thank You God"

CHAPTER IV

PRAYING IN SPIRIT AND IN TRUTH

"… Worship Him in Spirit and in Truth"   John 4:24

King James Version, Amplified Holy Bible, Zondervan, 1995

Wedding at Christ the Rock Church.

Chapter IV - Introduction: Standing Firm

Praying In Spirit and In Truth is a collection of prayers which were recorded during the period of 2001- 2010. These selected and intense prayers capture a time when I first began serving Jesus Christ in a ministerial position at Christ the Rock Church International, Brooklyn, New York, then, through my relocation to Orlando, Florida in 2006 and to the present where I am the Pastor of The Glorious Church of Christ in Orlando.

Prior to my 2001 commitment to church ministry, I had experienced dramatic and painful changes in my life. Shortly after receiving God's financial blessings and overall improvement in my life, I began a return to my lifestyle of pleasure. My relationship with God decreased and my involvement in cultural and social activities took precedent even over my family life. I performed my financial responsibilities and performed my household duties with my wife and sons but I left them at home because I became busy at nighttime with the social life of the culture.

Needless to say, I continued the normal pattern of social drinking and immoral living. All seemed well on the outside as my home was still at peace and comfortable, until, my family(my sons and my wife) decided that it was time to return to the United States. I supported the decision.

In 1999, when the time came to relocate, I was of two minds. I couldn't see myself leaving to start all over again. I was trapped in the present enjoyment of my lustful desires and the well paying position that I had. Although, I was supportive of the move, I had selfish motives. But, my wife and sons left and I remained to close off all transactions.

During this period alone, for the first time in over17 years, I reviewed my married life and realized that I was unhappy in my marriage. I did my duty but I lived unfaithfully. I was married but lived a separate life as an individual. I didn't know what I wanted. All I wanted then and there was to break free and to be romantically in love again. I had met someone whom I believed had the right heart to meet the present need of my heart and I was blinded to the responsibility of marriage.

Finally, I joined my family in the United States. We left our home and our jobs to start anew after being away for almost 11 years. As the months prodded along, I couldn't readjust smoothly because my mind was no longer comfortable with my wife's desires. There was a division and we couldn't agree. I was on another path while she was honest to our relationship. One day, I, summoned the courage to ask my wife for a divorce. This decision was not spontaneous but she granted it with some discomfort. I knew that I was hurting her and my sons. I held a meeting with my sons and I informed them of my decision. Thereafter, I returned to Trinidad and Tobago and to the company I worked for and to be near the person I had interest in and to be free to enjoy the pleasures of the culture.

However, in 2000, I became disenchanted with my life in Trinidad and I left for the U.S. to start over on my own. During my stay at my mother's house in Orlando, Florida, my girl friend was in England so I took the opportunity to visit her and my aunt Merle Miller, who hadn't seen me since I was a child. My aunt introduced me to Reiki, and I learned about this ancient Japanese system of natural healing through a process of attunements.

After that visit, I relocated to Brooklyn, New York and took up employment as a Social Studies Teacher in the NYC Public Schools. I also began attending church on a regular basis at Christ the Rock International where Dr. Rev. Jonathan and Dr. Rev. Olutoyin Owhe are the pastors. They are awesome spiritual leaders and are a biblically-based and spirit-filled husband and wife team from the nation of Nigeria in Africa.

However, on September 11th 2001, while teaching in the Bronx, I witnessed on television, the terrorists attacks on the World Trade Center with the use of highjack US American Airlines airplanes. This event shook me up and led me to search the Word of God for the meaning of the times. I wanted to know how God could use me because the times seemed dangerous and uncertain. In fact, this is what I presented to the Church as a testimony concerning the 9/11 attack on U.S. soil.

"Brothers and Sisters, When I watched those airplanes crashed into the World Trade Center, as a former military man, I knew we were at war. But, sadly, I also felt that America, this great civilization, was on the verge of falling!

When I saw the two twin towers fall, all the iron and brick crumbled like dust. I truly felt America was beginning to go the way as Egypt and Rome. So, I began to pray and asked God to reveal to me something so that I could prepare my mind, my body, and my spirit for this destruction that I saw unfolding before my eyes. Brothers and Sisters, when this attack on WTC took place, I was teaching 9, 10, and 11 year old children and they were scared. The adult teachers and staff were scared. But, I just began to explain that a war was on against our country and that we should think about what we will have to do come tomorrow. What would our lives be like tomorrow! What actions would America take tomorrow! Are we to prepare for war or do we act normal tomorrow? Who are these terrorists and where are they ?

Then, recognizing the fear and uncertainty, I began to talk about the innocent lives that were lost and the many more that may die tomorrow. But, God is good, because the children asked me to pray and I gathered them into a corner and we prayed for the dead, we prayed for the living and we prayed for a safer tomorrow. I prayed for them and for all of us to get home safely and that none of our parents or relatives were at that site at that time of this deadly attack within America. We were all surprised and we all needed hope."

That night, the Lord directed me to the book of Daniel chapter 4 verses 22, 23, 26 and 27. It stated the following:

"...You have become great and strong; your greatness has grown until it reaches the sky, and your dominion extends to distant parts

of the earth." V.22

**"… Chop down the tree and destroy it,
but leave the stump and roots in the earth,
bound with a band of iron and bronze …" v.23**

**"And inasmuch as they gave the command to
leave the stump and roots, your kingdom shall
be assured to you, after you come to know that
Heaven rules." v.26**

"… It may be then your prosperity will continue."v.27

This word from the Book of Daniel in the Old Testament reassured me that the American Civilization still had hope of arising out of the rapid decline that I initially and fearfully imagined. But, just as Daniel gave the King a warning about returning to God in order to prosper, so to I discerned that the political, economic, social and cultural leadership of the United States may have to "come to know that Heaven rules" in order that the country's "prosperity will continue." I prayed that the government would come to this knowledge and guide our nation safely through this damaging period.

Individually, with this revelation, I began to seek a deeper relationship with God so that He could become the ruler of my life and that I would be assured of His promised blessings here on earth and in heaven. In fact, the lord answered one of my request faster than I expected. In October 2001, one month, after the destructive attack and the unnecessary lost of thousands of innocent lives, I received the promise of His Spirit in my heart.

It all started when I was looking for a lamp for my night stand. One evening I was travelling on the bus on Malcolm X blvd. on Utica Avenue, in Brooklyn, a few blocks from my apartment when I saw a beautiful lamp stand. It was at a Church that sold use clothing and antique items. The seller wanted $10.00 for the item but I negotiated for $7.00 and I got it. The seller turned out to be the pastor. He asked me if I was a minister because he saw my leather case which held my Bible. I replied "no, just only a believer."

As I was about to leave, I saw an open Bible on a pulpit on the street among the clothes. It was opened on 1 Corinthians 14. I was surprised because I wanted to know more about tongues and how to receive it. After discussing this coincidence with him, he invited me into the church and poured oil on my head and laid hands on me and prayed for me. I had given him the permission because I had been asking God for this experience. I just cried as he prayed but nothing happened to me at that time. I took my night light and returned home in preparation for Friday night prayer at Christ the Rock International Church.

Later that evening at church, as Pastor Jonathan was ministering, one of the male members, who had been doing repair work on the church, ran into the sanctuary frantically pleading for prayer. The Pastor encouraged us to pray as he laid hands on the member. The man fell to the floor under the anointing. At this time, the Pastor opened the floor for prayers and many people came forward and were falling out. I had had Pastor laid hands on me before and I never fell so I wasn't going up but I was moved by the presence of God and I found myself on the line. As Pastor Jonathan touched me on my forehead, I fell to the floor. I was down for the first time in my life and I tried to get up because I felt a little embarrass but I couldn't. I just surrendered and laid out flat. As I did that, I started to feel a heat sensation flowing up and down my body, inside of me, and tears were flowing from my eyes and my mouth quivered and my tongue was moving as I was speaking and I was seeing people and places even though my eyes were closed, as I was in the spirit realm. Then, I heard Pastor Jonathan told someone to leave him there for awhile.

When I finally got up, there was no one in the church except for the pastor and a few ministers. I asked them what had happened and they told me that I was 'drunk' in the spirit and that I had spoken in tongues and that I was down for quite some time. They asked me to speak in this new language in order to confirm that it was true. I did. Then, they explained to me that it was not tongues that one should seek first but the baptism of the Holy Spirit first with the evidence of speaking in tongues.

I heard what they said but I was in a state of amazement. I felt like a deep seated miraculous experience had taken place inside of me. It was so overpowering that I couldn't stop it with my own strength or with my mind. I felt joyous, relieved and holy and in awe. I knew that something had happened to me beyond my control but it was godly and it was what I had been asking the lord to bless me with because I had read about it in the New Testament and I had heard Christian believers speak about it. And, now, my prayers had been answered.

When I returned to my apartment, I made a joke about it when I saw my lamp stand. I said, 'Today, I went looking for a light. I saw a light that I negotiated for $7.00 which I placed on my night table but tonight I got the 'true' light on the floor of the Church for free which God placed inside of me on the table of my heart.'

Thereafter, my life began to move more purposefully and my behavior seemed to be directed with a sense of meaning. I was no longer myself or seemed to be in control of myself. I just felt directed to absorb everything related to God. It seemed as though I was working with and for God and that I didn't have much time to devote to the things I use to do. It seemed as though I was speeding or trying to not waste any more time because I had a lot to learn and to do for God and I had to move quickly.

I had accepted Jesus Christ in 1976, was water baptized in 1989 and now, in October 2001, one month after 9/11, I got baptized in the Holy Spirit. I began to understand the Word of God with more clarity. My previous lifestyle of 'loose living', drugs and partying ceased to manifest in my life as I grew in the knowledge and wisdom of the teachings of Jesus Christ and the apostles. I had become very active in the church with the children, youth and men ministries and with the prayer and follow-up ministry. The Holy Spirit was developing a mind of Christ within me.

But, during this time, my personal friend had relocated to Brooklyn, N.Y. and eventually moved into my apartment and we were living together. We attended church together. Then one day, Pastor Jonathan called me to a meeting and informed me that my living arrangement was not in accordance with biblical teachings and the Christian way of life. I agreed but with reservations. He told me that as a leader in the church I needed to comply to God's ways in that area of my life or else he had to 'sit' me down from any leadership position in the church. I could attend but I could not lead. I agreed again and we made an arrangement to meet at an appointed time in order to discuss my relationship situation.

My friend and I had lived together in Trinidad for almost a year and now in Brooklyn we had been together for a couple of months. It was her first time in the U.S. and I was her support although she had relatives in this country. She attended church and had accepted Jesus Christ as Her lord and Savior at Christ the Rock Church International and she was growing in the Lord as well. When I told her of the decision by Pastor Jonathan, she understood but she cried. She was in a dependent situation. We agreed that I would 'sit' down from the leadership positions. We would attend church but refrain from looking as a couple and that as soon as she got employment and made enough money to cover the cost of an apartment she would move out. This was our prayer point and our plan.

I told the Pastor and I told my family and friends. Many of them disapproved of our plans. They thought that we were crazy. They felt that everyone knew that we loved each other and that we had been living together for a long time. I pained but I knew the truth and I wanted to stand firm on the truth of God's words. The Pastor was correct in his approach to leadership in the church.

Eventually, my friend found a job and she made enough to live on her own. We found a basement of a friend's house in Queens, NY and she moved in and paid her rent. We were separated in living quarters but we saw each other regularly and we attended church. I had a car and I picked her up and dropped her home. I told the Pastor about the separation but that I was thinking about getting married again. He made an appointed for us to attend counseling with him and his wife.

In the first session of counseling, I met individually with the pastor. He asked about my previous relationship and about my sons. I told him that divorce papers had been filed and that I had intermittent contact with my sons. That I prayed for peace and a closer relationship with my former wife and the boys. He indicated to me that I needed to clear up this situation before I could move forward. I had to contact my wife and to discuss with her if it was truly over and that we agreed and that I had to ask for forgiveness and to forgive her and that I had to seek forgiveness from my sons and to make peace with her and them in person or over the phone.

I knew that he was right. I knew that I had not settled my separation from my family sincerely in my soul. I knew that I had walked away out of my selfishness, sinfulness and insecurity. And, after becoming more knowledgeable about God's laws, I knew that confession and forgiveness releases the soul from all hurt, pain and wrong doing. I agreed to do it. I wanted to confront the truth of my life and to be honest with my reality. I wanted to cleanse my soul from all these sins. I wanted to be right with God. I was convicted within my soul and I wanted to be free.

One day upon returning to my apartment, my friend was with me but I couldn't help myself, I began to pray and to cry and to sob and to groan and I fell to the floor and I began pleading with the Lord, and with the Holy Spirit to help me to make this decision about my life and my future. I was confused. My past and my present had arisen together at this juncture of time and I had to bear my soul over my wife, my sons, my friend, my relationship with God and my work for Jesus Christ in the Church. I had to communicate personally my true feelings and I didn't want to evade it or run away from it. My friend prayed with me and encouraged me to do what was right. She said that she would agree with whatever decision I made and she left.

All that night I prayed and meditated on the word of God and I sought strength from the Holy Spirit to initiate this process of soul cleansing and renewal. I needed restoration and redemption from a darkened past and a clouded present which I accepted as my main doing. Then, with a guarded heart and an open mind, I made the telephone calls. I ask my wife for forgiveness and I forgive her. I discussed the situation and there were some hesitation but then there was agreement that we had moved on with our lives. My sons accepted and they never complained.

A few months later my wife told me that my younger son was graduating from High School. I attended his graduation in Orlando, Florida. My son was elated to see me at his graduation. Then, I took the opportunity to personally ask my wife for forgiveness and to forgive her. I did this over dinner. She accepted. My wife and I became friends. There was no hostility and hatred. We laughed and smiled over how we had matured and had grown even in our own personal relationship with the Lord.

I left Orlando feeling relieved, released and at peace with myself. I returned to Brooklyn and immersed myself in theological studies through an outreach program at the Church with Oral Roberts' University. My friend also attended the ORU adult program. We also attended several spiritual marital counseling sessions with the pastor and his wife. A few months later, after the divorced was final, I married my friend and my former wife also got married. I believed that God had given both us a second chance.

In 2004, I accompanied Pastors' Jonathan and Olutoyin Owhe and one other minister on a missionary journey to Sri Lanka and India. It was an extraordinary mission filled with trials and triumphs. The trials were delayed luggage, vehicle accident, long passport checks, unexpected change of flights and much more but the triumphs were the great and warmed welcome by the hundreds of people and the many pastors, the soul winning, the laying on of hands, the training programs and the educational materials and equipment distribution and the establishment of an Asian Headquarters of Christ the Rock International Church and many other activities.

I always wanted to visit India because of ancestral and spiritual reasons but I was overjoyed to have been there to share the gospel of Jesus Christ and to witness the growth of Christianity in Sri Lanka and India. It was an awesome experience for all of us. I recalled that my first utterance before the large Sri Lankan congregation was a song in tongues. I never sung in tongues openly before and I didn't planned it but it came out. The people gazed at me with amazement and they applauded with excitement at the conclusion. I believed that they were touched by the Holy Spirit who guided me as to what to say.

Upon our return to the U.S., I vigorously worked on completing my theological studies and by 2005 I had graduated with an advanced certificate in theology from ORU. This was a great achievement. Then, my wife, Tracy, gave birth to our daughter, Makeda. This was a great blessing. Then, added to that, I received another blessing as I was ordained as a Pastor by the Pastors and the Executive Board of the Church.

However, after one year of assisting in the pastoral capacity, I began to get an unction, that is, an inner tugging, to relocate to Orlando, Florida in order to be near my ailing mother and to be accessible to my sons. It was a constant battle of thoughts. I was performing my spiritual service, and I was growing in my relationship with the Lord. My wife was a part of the Church family. There was a genuine unity and friendship with the leadership. All was well except for this inner voice urging me to move on.

I told my wife that we had to leave very soon. She couldn't understand but she agreed. I told the pastors and they accepted. But, when I got all the household items on a trailer and I resigned from my responsibilities in the church, that's the moment that the tears and disbelief showed up. At our release ceremony, my wife cried again, the pastor's wife cried, the pastor said that he was releasing me but time will tell. The church members were both saddened and joyful at the same time. I held my position that what I had heard within me was not my imagination nor was it my desire to leave all behind especially when things were going good. I truly believed that it was the call of the spirit of God urging me to move nearer to my family in Orlando.

In 2006, we relocated to Orlando and lived with my mother and with my brother and with my younger son who also lived with my mom. Within three months, my wife and I were employed and we obtained a house three houses apart from my mothers'. We attended several churches and eventually I began to assist the Pastor, Rev. Dr. David Green at Mt. Olive AME Church in downtown Orlando. In 2007, my younger son had a spiritual conversion and he came to live with us. In the middle months of 2007, I began to ask God to put me to work full time for Him. Then, all of a sudden, I was filled with a passion to write a vision for a church that the Holy Spirit said was coming. I couldn't sleep until I wrote what He was dictating to me. I must have rewritten that vision over about ten times.

During that process, I felt the urge to resign from the Methodist Church. The Pastor had just mentioned to me that he was about to promote me to Superintendent of Church School. I told him that I couldn't accept the position because the Lord was leading me to open a church. I believe that he couldn't see what I saw and many didn't see it as possible when I told them. I, myself, didn't see it and I didn't know how it was going to happen but I knew within me that I needed to get ready for a church. So, I stepped out in faith and we started to have Worship and Bible Studies at our home.

Well, in June 2008, I was released from my teaching job due to budget cuts and the economic recession. And, by divine arrangement, two prophetesses confirmed that God wanted me to start a church in Orlando. Pastor Jonathan and I reconnected in New York when I went there to teach in the summer of 2008. He agreed to assist me in starting a branch of Christ the Rock Church International in Orlando. By September, we had a place and we moved our home services to this new site and I began to pastor this church with the help of my wife, younger son, mother and neighbors and friends. By December of 2008, my eldest son came to live with us in order to pursue a law degree. I came to understand that the call of the Holy Spirit in 2006 in New York to relocate to Orlando, Florida was real and that by my faithful obedience, He had blessed me not only with the nearness to my family but with both my sons and my daughter living and growing together in the same house. He also caused my mother and my brother to support me with the church, the same church that I told my former church leaders in 2007 that God said was coming. I was Pastor of this branch for one year until financial problems due to the economic recession forced a scale down in operations.

Immediately after this church's dislocation, I was blessed to start and pastor a new church which I was led by the Spirit to name, **The Glorious Church of Christ**. Our doors were opened in October 2009. We are small now but with the power of prayer, the guidance of the Holy Spirit and the authority of Jesus Christ and with the plan of God, the Father, we are confident that God will supply the provision and the workers to successfully accomplish what He has commissioned this church to do in Central Florida.

As you read the prayers, the thoughts and experiences in **Praying In Spirit and In Truth**, I encourage you to open your mind and to meditate on the words of these prayers, and if you discern any inspiration, let your heart respond to the call of the Holy Spirit and let the mind of Christ anoint the crown of your head and allow the light of His wisdom to shine on your forehead so that you can manifest His perfect will for your life through your faith and your actions. Or you can do as I did when Love first called me and I answered to the Spirit in me. You can surrender all of you, your spirit, soul and body and your possessions, your relationships and all your affairs into His loving care and allow

Him, the Lord Jesus Christ, the Messiah, the Savior, the Express Image of God, God's Divine Love to take care of you daily and forever. When you get to know Him in spirit and in truth, your thoughts, your feelings and your actions are your expression of His love. May you find that call by the Spirit as you read these writings and may you be motivated to seek Him in spirit and in truth just as Jesus Christ has asked us to do in the scriptures of the Bible.

Trevor C. Belmosa

Jesus Is God

Lord Jesus, You were born by the Word
of God. His Holy Spirit overshadowed Your
earthly mother, Mary, the virgin, and You, my
Savior, my redeemer, the Messiah, the Son of
God was divinely and humanly born.
God decreed that You come as it was written
In the volume of the books and as was spoken into the
Spirit of the wise.
Yes, God, the Father, loved us so much that He
wanted us saved. So, he sent You, out of Himself,
He released His divine nature into a pure human
womb and miraculously His fleshly image walked
on earth to bring light to a dying world.
Oh, Jesus of Nazareth, of the Jewish people, You
were crucified, for the world hated the truth which
You represented … the Word of God in the Flesh,
You were God living among human beings, God with us.
no impostor died on the cross! Yes, the story of You
is real both spiritually and historically and You were
more than a great teacher or prophet. You were God's
Righteousness on earth, alive, and in human form and
other human beings were seeing God, the Father, face to face,
for You were the Visible image of our invisible God.
Not limited to an inner voice, not limited to a burning bush,
not limited to a cloud by day or a pillar of fire by night,
not limited by a thundering voice, not limited by a shadow
of a back, not limited to a radiant light, not limited to a
hand writing on the wall, not limited as a fourth man in the
fiery furnace, not limited by man's fear. No! No one else
in the World were and are as You, Lord Jesus. God in the flesh.
Your crucifixion, Your death, is our victory over a
perishing people and world. Your shed blood is our
Lifeline which springs forth a new heaven and a new
earth within us and in time to come. We are no longer perishing
but our humanity has been made whole. Our divinity has been

reconciled with God's divinity within us
and around us because of Your love and sacrifice.
Lord Jesus, no one stole Your body out of the tomb
because God does not steal or lie for He is not a man
like us. A Creator has no reason to rob Himself of what
is His own creation. God's Spirit raised up the body of Jesus,
the same Spirit that overshadowed Jesus' mother.
O Lord, Your resurrection, what a glorious solution to Satan's
deception.
Human beings could see clearly now
That from dust to dust was not all there is but from spirit to spirit
was the greater call. Yes, my Father, God, You sent Jesus from
Yourself
and You received Jesus back to Yourself.
Now, He is seated on the throne on the right hand side.
Lord Jesus, we read about You, we talk about You, and
we accept You as our Lord and Savior and our Father knows that
we need to know where You are and so for our sake, the Father,
God, who has given us so much love,
has allowed His once fleshly now glorious body in the
image of His Son, Jesus, to share the throne in Heaven so that we
can, as fleshly beings,
continue to reach out to You the way we once saw You,
when You walked the earth as a human being just as us.
We, too, have the hope and the faith to become as You, a glorified person.
You came as Jesus to show us the way, the truth and the life.
God, we know that You were Jesus and that Jesus is Your body.
Jesus is the earthly and divine substance of You, God.
For Jesus is God.
Thank You for loving us, human beings, so much,
and, for revealing Yourself to us in human form.
Your truth will prevail and Your love will never fail!
For Jesus is God when you think about what God looks like.
In Jesus Name, Amen.

Trevor C. Belmosa

Heal Your Temple

Holy Spirit move in me and stir up my creativity.
It is You, O, Spirit of God who leads and guide
me daily. Yes, Holy Spirit, You remind me daily
of my Lord and Savior Jesus Christ. You make me
aware of God, my Father and Creator all the time.
I am confident that all three of You are one and the
same; One loving and merciful God. One essence
of existence but just three manifestations, three
functions, and just three personalities all wrapped
up in one precious gift of love residing in the world
and within me, in my temple.
Oh, How my temple need Your mercy right now?
O, Jesus, in thy kingdom have mercy upon me. O,
Jesus, Son of David have mercy upon me. I plead
the blood of Jesus over my temple and by his stripes
I am healed. I am healed of my hearing loss. I am
healed of my swollen jaw. I am healed of my sinus
and respiratory illness. Yes, Lord, I am healed by
Your blood, in my upper body, my brain and all over
my body where there is pain.
O, Holy Spirit, O, Father, God, O Jesus, thank You,
Lord. This body is Your temple … clean it, purify it,
anoint it, and get it readied to be filled with Your healing
power. Come God reign in this temple. Root out all
sickness, infirmities, disease, unclean spirits, false thoughts
and evil strongholds! Cut loose any demonic spirits encamping
around this temple and take charge of my temple. Work Your work
and move in Your might. I surrender this temple into Your care.
Heal Your temple, In the name of Jesus Christ, Amen.

You Stretched My Giving

Father, God, I thank You for teaching me
to sow financial seeds, to be a giver.
You have stretched my giving at this time
and You have broken me out of my normal
tithing and offering pattern.
Father, You have caused me to give more
than before and You have given me the vision
to open my mind to receive. I have stepped
out in faith knowing that my sowing will bring
me a harvest from Your unlimited
abundance.
Lord Jesus, as I take this sowing of financial
seed beyond my normal status quo, I am confident
that a new trend, a new financial outlook, a new
financial breakthrough has taken place first within
me and surely in all areas of my life.
Father, in the name of Jesus, I thank You for allowing
me to willingly pour out this extra money into the
Kingdom of God, into building a new church where
Your words and Your ways will be established and
the head of Satan will be crushed.
Holy Spirit, I thank You for guiding me in holy obedience
to God's Word on sowing financial seeds, of tithing 10%
and giving more in addition to the tithe at this time. You have stretched
my giving and I am grateful because You always remind me
that giving is the key to receiving.
So, Father, God, as You stretched me today in my giving
I now stretch my preparedness, my readiness to receive
more than what You guided me to give. Yes, Lord,
a hundredfold is coming to me now! I praise You, Lord.
I honor You and You deserve all my thanks. As I give to You,
to Your work, I know my health, wealth, success and happiness
is guaranteed. It is Your spiritual law and it will always fulfill
its purpose. I can't wait to celebrate my increase from my tithing.

Trevor C. Belmosa

I know that tithing is the spiritual basis for my spiritual inheritance of abundance.
From my loving Father who desires to prosper me in my lifetime.
In the Name of Jesus, Amen.

Billions of Souls Walking In

Get ready for billions of souls are coming
before the King of Glory.
Yes, the worldwide harvest is ripe and billions
of souls are walking into the Kingdom of God
and believers of Christ are planting the Gospel
of Jesus on top of the roof of the globe.
It has been foretold, Go forth!
In the Power of the Lord! And baptize billions
of lost souls in the Name of the Father and of the Son,
and of the Holy Spirit!
The trumpet has sounded within the Churches …
open the doors… and breathe the Word of God
into all dry bones!
Arise! the King of Kings and the Lord of Lords,
the bridegroom of the Glorious Church commands…
Be faithful to the mission of the commission … Go, Now!
Release the Power of the Living Word!
Release the Power of Faith!
Release the Power of Prayer!
Release the Power of Giving!
And, Stand Still, Open your Eyes, and See,
Billions of souls forgiven and free walking out of blindness
and misery into the majesty of the Almighty!
Fear not! But Rejoice! For it is the planting of the Lord.
It is His billions of souls becoming His trees of righteousness.
Just Let Go, and Let them walk into His garden of eternal life.
In the Name of Jesus, Amen.

Become A son To The Father

I submitted myself to Jesus Christ and I have become a son to the Father.

And, Now, I have access to all my Father's promises and blessings.

I am Joint-Heir with Christ and the fullness of the Father dwells in me.

I don't lean on my own understanding and my confidence is not in my own ability. I don't try to work things out on my own but I draw on the wisdom and guidance of my Father.

I have come to the full revelation of who I am in Christ and I trust in the ability of my Father to bring to pass that which he has ordained for my life.

I know that my Father loves me because He has begotten me by His Spirit and He has birthed me by the blood of Jesus Christ. I am saved and I am free because I am His son.

I am rising up to take my rightful place as a true son of the living God, Who is my Father.

I release my mind from thoughts of fear, doubt and worry because I know that my Father has already given me the victory over Satan through Christ Jesus.

I walk in power and authority over sin, over my flesh and over demons because my body is the home, is the temple of my Father.

And, He has anointed my head with the 'Crown of Christ' and He has put His hand on my forehead and released the 'Mind of Christ' in me.

And, I am being taught all things in truth as He abides in me.

And, as a son to my Father I know it is His pleasure to give me the Kingdom.

It is His pleasure to see me prosper.

So, my mind and my spirit is open to receive all of my Father's gifts.

I am ready to receive all of the lavish abundance He has for me.

He has given me unlimited access to His supernatural and natural provisions in order to meet every need. I receive them freely and I freely give as my Father directs, to the church, to the poor, to the sick and to the needy.

I pray. I teach and preach His Word. I serve. I give and I give thanks because my Father treats me as His son more so when I submitted myself to Jesus Christ.

I encourage you to become a son to the Father. Just accept Jesus Christ as Your Lord and Savior. You will be blessed. Become a son to the Father and you'll see, the power of His grace, mercy and favor in your life!

In Jesus Name, Amen.

Trevor C. Belmosa

A Prayer For My Wife and Daughter

Praise the Lord! He is worthy to be Praised,
He alone is God.
I thank You, Lord, For finding a good wife for
Me, for ordering her footsteps into my path, and
for inspiring me to see the goodness of her heart.
Lord, Now, we are one flesh in Christ Jesus, in
marriage, which You honor and which You promised
to release Your favor.
I thank You, Lord, that You are the source of her
Life, that she is identified in Your righteousness,
in Your death, in Your resurrection and in Your
glorification.
You saved her and poured Your Holy Spirit within
her and cleanse her of all her sins. You are truly an
awesome God.
Lord, let Your blood cover her totally and rebuke all
danger, hurt, pain and demonic attacks against her and
destroy all evil strongholds in her life.
Let her prayers be answered and keep her in Your love
and eternal sanctuary when she sits and bows at Your
feet, at the throne of our Father.
Thank You, Lord, that, at times, we pray, hand in hand,
together touching and agreeing and becoming one voice,
one presence, one flesh, in one accord before Your altar,
asking forgiveness of our sins, of our weaknesses and our
transgressions against each other, against our children, our
family, friends, strangers, co-workers, business partners and
against You, too, Lord.
Lord, as we pray for guidance, strength and to be good stewards
of all Your blessings in our lives, we will never lose sight of
Who You are in our marriage.
You are the centerpiece of our togetherness, whether, in good
and bad times, in season or when the season doesn't look right.
Lord, as she prays for our daughter, her physical joy, let Your
Perfect joy and peace fill her within and let it flow out to cover

her daughter's entire lifespan.
Let our daughter walk forever in Your will and Your ways.
Save our daughter and use her for Your kingdom.
Reveal Your divine plan for our daughter very early in her life.
Let her prosper in all areas of her life. Let Your miracles, signs and
wonders follow her.
Lord, Let Your will be done in my wife's life. Holy Spirit comfort,
counsel, and empower her to be the best she can be in her
generation. Jesus, break every generational curse upon her and
her family and use her as a shining light to her family and friends.
Lord, Jesus, Release Your wealth, divine health, ministry, prosperity
and Your fullness within her and make her a blessing to others.
Thank You, Lord, for blessing her and lifting her out of darkness
and adding her name to the many names on the pages in the
Book of Life. She's Yours, Lord! Have Your way in her life.
Manifest Your power and Your glory within and around her and
give her the desires of her heart,
and keep me loving her and her loving me as she follows You,
Lord, above all else. Thank You, Jesus, for loving her and for giving
me this precious wife and lovely daughter through her. Thank You,
In Jesus Name, Amen.

Trevor C. Belmosa

Women of My Family

Lord, give me the strength to fight this war.
To confront the enemy with boldness, authority,
and decisiveness on behalf of the women in my
family.
Lord, I lift up my mother and I pray that by Your
Stripes she is healed of all diseases and pain. By
Your Blood, restore her to good health. In Your Name,
I build a hedge of protection around her and I rebuke
the devourer from her presence.
Lord, I pray that You release financial blessings into
her life and that You make her environment peaceful
and joyful and let her mind be at peace and her heart
be comforted.
And, Lord, let her fulfill the purpose You made her
come into this life to accomplish. Let her sharing and
caring be not in vain.
Thank You, Jesus, for loving my mother and for saving
her through Your eternal grace and mercy.
Lord, Jesus, look upon my sister. Cover her with Your
Blood and renew within her an inner joy and rejoicing.
Protect her and her household from the wicked tricks of
the devil. Rebuke spiritual fear and loose peace, goodness
and prosperity into her home ... let Your harmony and glory
prevail in her life. Thank You, Jesus, for giving her salvation.
Right now, Lord, I lift up every woman in my family, those
saved and unsaved.
Holy Spirit, I implore Your comfort, counsel and truth to
caress them and convict them to increase their faith and to
humble themselves at the feet of Jesus Christ.
Holy Spirit, Let them accept Him as their Head, their authority,
their covering and instruct them to serve Him.
Lord, Jesus, heal all sicknesses, diseases, addictions, fornication,
adulteries, and sins in their lives. Purify them from all abuses, rape,
abortions, barrenness, low self-esteem, poverty, instability, insecurity,
crisis of identity and generational curses.

And, pour Your love, Your salvation, Your anointing, Your
sanctification, and Your resurrection power upon them.
Release Your living waters into their lives and empower them
to worship You, to know You through the Word of God and to
spread Your Gospel throughout their generations.
Lord, let every woman in my family prosper and bring happiness
and godliness into her home and teach her children the ways of Jesus
Christ.
Let them become 'one flesh' with their husbands, let them be fruitful
joint-heirs and help-mates of righteousness.
And above all, let them love their husbands and receive love and respect
from their husbands.
And, may they always love their mothers and fathers regardless of good
or bad experiences and rise above all challenges.
Thank You, Jesus, for bringing forth godly and spirit-filled women
in my family. In Jesus Name, Amen.

Trevor C. Belmosa

I Walk In Freedom

I walk free with the knowledge of You, Lord, and
I'm not turning back.
No, the enemy and his fleshly evil ways are under
my feet, and You, Jesus, have won the victory.
Lord, You, have freed me! No man can free me!
No person can emancipate my mind but Jesus Christ.
He renewed and transformed my mind by His Word,
His Love, His Sacrifice, His Resurrection and His
Ascension.
Jesus has given me the power and the authority to be
the leader and not the follower; to be the owner and not
the renter; to be the giver and not the borrower; to rule
the land and not to be a slave of the land.
Freedom! Freedom! God has set me free.
God has written the true emancipation proclamation on
my heart and His Words are the constitution that I follow.
So slavery, oppression, bigotry, hatred, evil, poverty, failure,
fear and insecurity, all of you, are dead in me. Be buried forever
in the name of Jesus!
I have been blessed. The Holy Spirit of God touched my spirit
And cleanse me from sin and shame. He gave me the gift of
eternal life. I belong to God's kingdom. I am a child of Christ
and that's why I walk in freedom. I have the mind of Christ and
I wear the crown of His glory.
My body is the temple of His Spirit and all pain and hurt I count
it all gain for the freedom that no one can take away from me.
I am free! I walk in freedom. For whom the Son has set free,
is free indeed! Falsehood, ignorance and death have departed
and truth, wisdom and life have been quickened in me and
now I walk in freedom!
In Jesus Name, Amen.

God Is More Than You See

God, You do exist. You are alive. You created life
and You are greater than nature, history, philosophy,
science and psychology.
You are highly lifted up and Your handy work is in
everything.
You arrange for purpose and meaning to operate in
All things on earth.
You are beyond us and yet so very near to us, even
within us.
Surely, You are not like a man or a woman who has
need of food, clothing and shelter or desires for security,
a sense of belonging or self-actualization?
Nor are You like us that You need counseling or salvation.
You are the source and supplier of all life.
You are our redeemer, deliverer and liberator through
Your Son, Jesus Christ.
Lord, God, we cannot even comprehend all of Your
Creation and even Your intervention in it, except, in
parts and as You allow time to reveal yourself to us.
But, You know everything about us and our world in
totality.
Your Spirit moved on the earth and life was established
and You moved in us and directed our walk in faith, our
understanding of the truth and our salvation through
Your Word.
Father, our limited mind cannot begin to fathom Your
infinite existence. You are unlimited and You are beyond
the age of reason and reasoning.
Logic cannot define how Jesus Christ, though no longer
in the flesh, still touches and transforms so many souls,
sometimes, in a moment's cry.
You are greater than the ruler of this earth and all his evil
spirits who spread lies and falsehood.
You are more efficient than modern technology and
safer than laser radiation and satellite communication.

Trevor C. Belmosa

Lord, God, Your blessing is everlasting and Your
healing is supernatural but affects the natural.
Lord, You are alive so that we may know that we are
more than flesh and that this earth is not our only
destination.
Lord, we praise Your holy name, for You are worthy
to be praised. Your ways are higher than ours and Your
thoughts are greater than ours. And, Jesus Christ, whom
You sent, is the greatest solution to the human problem.
He is the revealer of the intentions of our hearts and
the visible image of You, our invisible God, our loving Father.
All we have to do is to read His Word and call on His Name
and you will know that God is more than what you can see.
You can hope in Him and believe in Him and ask Him to manifest
all that you need and it will come into your sight and you will be
pleased that He is more than you can see. Even the blind know that
God is more than you see. Just believe and see for yourself!
In Jesus Name, Amen.

Spirit of God

Spirit of God kind and true, let Your power
rain down upon me through and through,
Like the blood of my Savior, cleansing my
old behavior
and making me new, even while
You still chastise me to pay my due, including
my tithes and offering too.

Merciful Father, I praise Your Name, for You
have given me more favor than fame. You have
lifted me up above my circumstances, and showed
me that Your power and glory are beyond my
human senses.

Jesus, My King and Lord, I'll follow You and
surrender my all.
Take control of my heart so that Satan must depart,
And, I can truly play my part, in building Your kingdom,
on Earth,
before my body returns to dirt.

Holy Spirit of God and messenger of eternal love,
release Your dove,
of righteousness from above, within me,
because this world's ugliness and wickedness,
need to bow,
to my Lord's holiness and loving kindness,
which I long for all to see, operating fully
as the Spirit of God in our earthly reality.

He Revealed To Me His Son

Lord, You, have revealed to me my nothingness, my brokenness, emptiness, powerlessness and that I have no substance of my own. Who am I and what am I without You Lord? Have I any control and power over my life? Am I not a mere man who stands naked and devoid of purpose who awaits impending death without You?

Lord, out of the tears from my eyes, heart, mind and soul, You revealed to me, Your presence, Your Son, Jesus Christ, my Savior, the One who is the door that I can open and enter through to Your kingdom and be Saved from wrongdoing.

You showed me that Your Son can transform my unproductive, purposeless, meaningless, wasteful and destructive lifestyle. O Jesus, forgive me, forgive me for all those years of not listening to Your voice, Your call, Your purpose, Your sacrifice for me. How blind could I have been? How foolish and ignorant could I have been to think that I was in charge of my destiny?

Jesus, You are the true Messiah; The true image of the living God. Only You alone can give us entrance into and exit out of our Fathers' mansion; into that glorious spiritual house of our God. You alone can give us permission to find peace, joy, righteousness and prosperity.

Thank You, Jesus, for sanctifying me, for wiping away my tears of sorrows and for empowering me with Your knowledge, counsel and might. You have reconciled me to God and healed me of my guilt and shame. You are my Restorer. You restored my hope and my relationship with my Father, the creator of all things in heaven and earth.

What an awesome gift You have given me? You have bestowed upon me eternal life and You removed my unworthiness. You have given me a life beyond death and my nakedness has been clothed with Your garment of praise and thanksgiving.

My spirit rejoices for You have made my purpose clearer.
You have discarded the veil of indecisiveness and You have lifted me
up ... up to Jesus ... up to the remembrance of His mighty works
and His call upon me ... to follow Him, to seek Him daily, to ask
Him for blessings, and to abide in His teachings, and to live by faith
in Him.

O Jesus, Your words are light to my life. I feel the power of truth
and wisdom in Your words and I now see that You are the Word.
Because, the Spirit of the Word has set my spirit free. Yes, I am
free in Jesus Christ! I am not myself anymore. I just know that
through Jesus, I belong to God. I am experiencing a molding and a
shaping that is not of my own doing. I believe that something good
happens when the love and mercy of God comes into your life. Oh,
how I love God for revealing His Son to me.

Imagine, God has called me to a higher purpose and a deeper walk
with Him which He said was ordained for my life and which had
nothing to do with my education, skills, or wealth. Just think,
the living God who created all of us called me by the spirit in me
that I didn't even know was the real me and convinced me that
Jesus Christ is love and He reigns supreme.

I am so grateful for the vision that He has given me of our Father's
kingdom that I pray that God will bless me more and more and that
He will bless you, too, who read this prayer. I pray that He gives you
wisdom to know the truth and to reveal His Son, Jesus Christ to you
just as He did for me through His Holy Spirit. I did nothing to deserve it.
He revealed His Son to me because He loved me and He wants me to
share this gift of love with others. I pray that you receive the Son of
His love too. In Jesus Name, Amen.

Trevor C. Belmosa

Under The Crown of Jesus

In the mighty name of Jesus Christ,
I pray a hedge of protection around
all my family members in the East,
West, North and South of the globe.

I pray that all my relatives will be
washed with the blood of Jesus and
that the Holy Spirit will minister to
them and direct them to the altar of
joy, peace, righteousness, holiness
and prosperity.

I pray that their lives will be
transformed and that all of them
will be in one accord under the
crown of Jesus Christ.

I pray that He will satisfy all of them
according to their specific needs and
that He will release His miracles, signs,
and wonders in their lives in order to
draw them into His kingdom.

I pray that the Holy Spirit of Jesus will
send forth His voice to awaken all my
family members who are sleeping in
the traps of sin and speak freedom into
their hearts and guide them to the
waterfall of His eternal stream where
they can drink from the fountain of
His living waters and never thirst again.

I pray that all my family members in
my generation and generations to come
will remain in the presence of the Lord,
under the crown of Jesus, and bask in
the glory of His majesty, at the feet of
His throne here on earth and in heaven.
In Jesus Name, Amen.

Forgive My Adulteries

Lord Jesus, Holy Spirit, Father, this morning
I cast all my burdens on Your table of strength.
I cast my sins, weaknesses, faults and un-forgiveness
into Your outstretched hands.
Lord, in the name of Jesus, cleanse me, forgive me
and help me.
Help me to be righteous before You. Cause me to
think like You,
to talk like You and to walk in truth, righteousness
and holiness, as You do.
Father, I place my sins of adultery, deceit, jealousy,
insecurity, drinking, smoking, going to the clubs,
and idolization of sex before Your altar of forgiveness.
Accept my imperfections! I surrender these known
sinfulness of mine before You, Lord.
Jesus, I cannot seem to overcome on my own,
with my own understanding or with my above-average
intellect. I stop for a while then I go back and do them
all over again.
I am weak! Please Jesus, work them out with me.
I need Your help.
I ask forgiveness for myself and for all the people,
including my former wife and children, whom I hurt
with my wrong thinking and behavior, with my lustful
way of living which I thought was culturally normal
because I didn't truly know You and the consequences
of not living within Your laws.
Lord, I petition You to heal each of us, to pardon each
of us for sinning against You and for being trapped in
this bondage of selfish pleasure and for violating the
vows of my marriage.
Jesus, I ask for Your tender mercy and loving kindness
in this situation. I release the guilt, the deceit, the
ignorance, the blindness and all the related sins I have
done against You.

Please, Holy Spirit, guide me, teach me, give me the
wisdom and understanding to hear the Father's voice,
to see Jesus' answer to these grave sins, blockages,
and barriers which have become a crisis and which have
caused a break-up in my family life.
Lord, touch our hearts, elevate our spirit, give us clarity
and show us unconditional love so that we can do what
is right and pleasing in Your sight. Explain Your truth to
us during this painful period in our destiny, and, God,
Just have Your way!
All I ask is that this mountain of despair be moved out
of my life in the Name of Jesus. Thank You, Lord,
for leveling the mountain of sins and for defeating this
evil spirit of lustfulness and for giving us victory over
spiritual death.
Lord, You are so wonderful, so marvelous. Your Word
and Your works have given life and healing to my
brokenness, emptiness, mental confusion and emotional
instability. You have restored me and You forgave me
and You made me well again. You gave me a
second chance. And everyone connected has been made
free by our forgiving of each other and by being cleansed
by Your blood, and, now, we can all walk without
condemnation and we can all respect and love each other
because of You, Lord, Jesus Christ.
Lord, I lift up Your Name. I exalt You with a great shout.
I give You the glory and all the praise. For You have
taken me through the mourning, through the separation,
through the divorce which I now know You hate. Yet,
You worked in me a marvelous and miraculous work
beyond my comprehension. You have taken away
the shame and You gave me a peace that quieted the storm.
What a joy! What a second chance? What great grace and
mercy of the Lord? Holy Spirit, Thank You. The Lord is
great beyond greatness. He is loving beyond love.
He has treated me better than I have treated myself.
Thank You, Jesus, for being the solid Rock of my salvation.

Trevor C. Belmosa

Now that I know Your ways, I will sin no more against You,
willfully. Thank You for forgiving me and for removing the
sins of my adulteries and all the pain I have caused to others.
I cried out to You and I repented and You set me free.
I love You, Lord, with all my heart. In Jesus Name, Amen.

Take Our Hands, Lead Us

Take my hand Lord and lead me on Your path of righteousness
and holiness
Let me be a shining example of Your glory
Bestow upon me the crown of Your suffering and the power
of Your might.
For I am Your servant, Lord, who stands ready to be led on to
the battlefield to destroy the strongholds of Your enemies
Let their unrighteousness and injustice bow before You. O, Lord,
Let Your power eliminate those satanic forces who are causing
hardships, doubts, fear, instability and bankruptcy.
O, Lord, let us drive out hopelessness and homelessness, disease
and disaster, death and destruction, anger, frustration and hatred
from in us, around us and from off the earth.
O, Father, You are a true Commander of war,
Come, take our hands and lead us into the arena of warfare
where we can conquer our foes and declare our victory certain.
Then, Lord, let the fruits of Your Spirit, the sanctuary of Your
infinity and Your favor of an everlasting pasture of a hundredfold
and a thousand-fold be our sweet reward.
So, Lord, Come! Take our hands and lead us, because, in these
troubled times, we need Your leadership. In Jesus Name, Amen.

Prayers For My Sons and Men In My Family

Lord, You are our true model of manhood. You said that You
will never leave us nor forsake us.
You are truly a Father who cares, who is committed and who
accepts the responsibilities of fatherhood.
Lord, today, I pray for my sons and all the men in my family.
Men whom You love But men who have not loved You as You
desired because the issues of life have trapped them and they are
torn between righteousness and lustfulness, between surrendering
to Jesus Christ and enjoying only what the world presents.
Lord, the lack of knowledge and revelation of Who You are and
Your standards have left the men in my family in the strongholds
of infidelities, adulteries, deception, mental illness, drug addictions,
alcoholism, domestic violence, imprisonment, financial instability,
low self-esteem and a distorted reality of manhood.
Lord, although on the outside all may look well in all areas of their
lives in their own understanding, but just open the hearts of their
spirits and allow the manliness of Jesus Christ to baptize them
and transform them into men of faith, into men of prayer,
into warriors against wickedness, into disciplined, committed,
loving and spirit-filled sons, brothers, husbands, fathers and spiritual
leaders, from within themselves, especially, and then in their homes.
Lord, Jesus, Heal the men of my family quickly. Let the blood that
flowed from Your beaten and bruised body cleanse and root out all
the diseases, abuse, rape, jealousy, insanity, pornography, crisis of
sexual identity, pride, lustfulness and generational curses that plague
them as men.
Then, Lord, plant the power of the Holy Spirit and the Word of God
into their hearts and anoint all the males with Your love and courage,
boldness, wisdom, and discernment. Holy Spirit, show the men in
my family how to bow down and worship God, how to praise Him
and to serve only Him with all their soul, spirit and body and with
their finances.
Teach them through Your divine revelation and Word that it is only
when they are in Christ and Christ is in them, then, and only
then, will they become 'real' men, men who follow the highest

standards of heavenly and earthly excellence. Then, they will truly become sons of the living God and filled with His abounding love. And, Lord, protect every male seed in my family in this generation and the generations to come. Capture every one of them with Your salvation and instruct them how to become outstanding stewards of Your manifold gifts and blessings which You placed in their lives. Lord, I thank You for saving me, for pouring Your Holy Spirit in me and for using me to pray for my sons and the men in my family, and, for my father before he died. I am a man surrendered into Your care to be perfected as an honorable vessel.

As You work on me, I know where You took me from. So I pray and I thank You, Lord, Jesus, in advance, for releasing all the men in my family from the bondage of sin and for directing our foot steps towards the true path of Manhood, Fatherhood and Servant-hood which only You represent. Lord, I thank You for making the men in my family men of Christ who will lead their families, their children, in prayer, in worship, in Bible Studies, in Church fellowship, in tithing and in serving and living for God in all areas of their lives. Teach them to love their wives as they love themselves. And, Father, cause the men never to curse their mothers or fathers but show them how to forgive their mothers and fathers and to love them always that they may live in peace and prosperity in all the generations of my family.

In Jesus Name, Amen.

Trevor C. Belmosa

Heal Me, Lord

Lord, Jesus, I come before You in pray and in tears
because this mortal body of mine is not well.
I'm in pain and I have fear because my life seems
uncertain and no one knows how I feel deep inside.
I'm tired of the medications, of the doctor's visits,
Hospital beds, the patient care and the enormous costs
for treatments.
Lord, I know that I have no right to be angry with You
or to blame You for my pain or impending death. But, I
will never quit, never give up or give in as those who
become impatient and cynical. Like those who refuse to
believe in You and turn away from You and not even pray
to You because their diseases and infirmities beat upon
their bodies unrelentingly.
Despite my hurting, You have taught me and I have learned
That You had healed me the moment I had accepted Jesus
Christ as my Savior. Because You awakened Your wisdom
within me and renewed my hope and faith in a God who loves
me even though I am sick and weak in my flesh.
You showed me that I'm more than my body and that You
have a home for me that is not made from human hands.
You restored my strength because Your Word promised that
it is possible, through Your grace and mercy, for my body to be
healed of its suffering, right now, or at Your appointed time, today
or tomorrow.
And, I believe You, Lord. For this is the greatest healing gift You
have given me, Salvation. So, I pray and I cry but I understand, that,
You are the author and finisher of my destiny and I thank You
for healing me, today, tomorrow or after my body dies and I live
in my glorious body before Your presence.
I have accepted Your Son, Jesus Christ, as my Savior and Lord
as Your Word commanded us to do, and I know You will make me
well.

You will heal me, soon, in due time. I speak healing over my body with Your words. And, I wait patiently even in pain because I know You care for me and will remove the tears, the hurt, the pain and the suffering. I believe totally in You and Your goodness.

In the Name of Jesus Christ of Nazareth, Amen.

Trevor C. Belmosa

Your Infinity

Lord, from infinity to infinity Your presence abounds
and Your Spirit roams and the Angels and the saints
gather before You, before Your royal majesty and glory.

Lord, You rule supreme in the Universe.
You are beyond the Universal Mind and Oneness of all
things. Karma and reincarnation and bliss are silent before Your truth
You are the Source and the Supplier.
You are divine in divinity and You are beyond measure,
beyond expression and understanding.
Wisdom bows before You and our spirits dance to a mere
spark of Your illuminating Spirit.

Lord, You are the consuming fire and the voice in the cloud.
You are boundless and limitless and the moon and star wait on
You. Your presence among us are like raindrops of holiness which
soaks our prayers with streams of love and heals our wounded
and broken spirit, mind and body.

Lord, Your radiance is like waves of energy that pushes us
deeper into the ocean of Your holy of holies which overflows into
our destiny and kindles our creativity to define Your creation.
Oh, What a human curiosity to seek after Your infinity without
accepting Your divinity and humanity? Lord, atoms, neutrons and
electrons and nuclear fissions are microscopic byproduct of Your
infinity.

And, technology is only a visible manifestation of relativity but we still
need Your guidance in order to fathom Your absolute unfathomable
majestic infinity.

Pray and Live by Faith

O, Heavenly Father, Master Jesus Christ, Divine Holy Spirit thank You for another day, another morning, another evening, another night, to praise You, to exalt You and to magnify Your Name.

Lord, I pray to You for more faith, more than I was born with. Holy Spirit increase my faith in Jesus Christ. Strengthen my belief in Him, the Son, of the living God. Give me faith beyond measure, pressed down, shaken together and flowing into me like rivers of waters.

Oh, Lord, just let my faith overflow with love, joy, peace and confidence in Jesus Christ, my Savior and Redeemer.

Lord, this morning, Your gift of faith has blessed me deep within my heart and my lips just responded with words of praises all day long.

Lord, Your faithfulness has magnified my faith and the Name of Jesus Christ has come alive with greater power within me.

This day is a beautiful day of faith. I will pray and live by faith in Jesus Christ, until the end of my days. In Jesus Name, Amen.

Trevor C. Belmosa

Speak, Holy Spirit

Your words are medicine to my heart Holy Spirit.
What You said gave my spirit voice to pray when
there were no words coming forth.
I was able to pray in tongues, in the spirit, and Your
presence lifted me and encouraged me to speak aloud.

Holy Spirit, Spirit of God, You are a mighty weapon which
shields, protects, and allows Jesus' voice to reach me and
to inspire me to pray. You, Holy Spirit, navigated my prayers
safely through the realm of invisible conflicts, and delivered
them straight to the altar of God's sanctuary.

Holy Spirit, You are so helpful, so comforting, and so caring,
I can always trust You and depend on You.
For what You said and did was truly a revelation and guidance
to my heart because my health improved and I was made well.
My prayers were answered immediately.

Thank You, Holy Spirit, for speaking to me when I couldn't
pray as I should and for reminding me to use my gift of tongues,
my spiritual language, to talk to God. You are truly my helper,
Holy Spirit, and, I thank You, again, for speaking to me.
In Jesus Name, Amen.

Clean My Tongue

Lord, take my tongue and soak it in the blood
of Jesus and wash off all the evil, hurtful, negative
and obscene words that my tongue said to injure
people and to speak death and curses into their lives.

Lord, dip Your finger into the cup of Jesus' blood
and use Your blood stained finger as a brush to scrub away
all the filthy and poisonous things my tongue said that was
not of faith and that was an abomination to Your ears.

Lord, lift my tongue from out the bowl of Jesus' blood
and use Your living waters as a water hose to spray off
all the impurities and toxins stored within my tongue.

Lord, use the power of Your blood to subdue this unruly
tongue which is so easily provoked to speak evil and so
ready to retaliate with vile words. Then, chastise my tongue,
circumcise my tongue, purify and sanctify my tongue from all
its profanity, nastiness, lies, slander, backbiting, and gossips.

Lord, sprinkle the holiness of Your blood on my tongue and
allow deliverance and salvation of my tongue to manifest.
Then, anoint, empower and command my tongue to speak positive,
wonderful, encouraging, comforting and motivating words into
peoples' lives.

Lord, thank You, for saving my tongue from a sinful life and for
giving it the fruit of self-control to remain silent when provoked
but to speak confidently, boldly, and forcefully with knowledge
and with wisdom about justice and peace. Lord, baptize and
spirit-fill my tongue to speak Your Holy Words, Your truth,
Your way and Your life and Your blessings into peoples' lives
without fear.
Thank You, Lord Jesus, for using Your blood to make my rebellious
and unclean tongue clean.
In Jesus Name, Amen.

Be Gone Lustful Thoughts and Dreams

Forgive us Lord for thoughts, imaginations and dreams
which are lustful and sexual, and have tempted us when we sleep.
God, We need Your strength and courage to bind these demonic
impressions which are attempting to entice us to sin in our dreams,
in our mind and in our flesh.
Holy Spirit, guide us to pray the prayer to subdue these deceiving
spirits and to destroy their unlawful influences upon our dreams.
Let us wake up while dreaming of these unclean imagery and cast
them out of our sub-conscious mind or let us rebuke them while we
sleep.
Lord Jesus, renew our vision, capture our imagination and bring
all ungodly thoughts into Your Holy obedience.
Lord, supply us with the weapons to fight in this spiritual battle against
these wandering foes. Put on us Your whole armor of
protection so that we can boldly confront their sexual raids on our
mind while we are unconscious.
Satan! You are a liar! Jesus Christ is the ruler of our lives.
We are a new creation in Christ! He has blessed us with His godly
nature.
That's why we know your tricks and subterfuge. Your lustful and
perverted methods of bombardment against the thoughts and dreams
of the faithful sons and daughters of God are shameful and
violent and terroristic.
Your demonic agents cast persuasive illusions during our sleeping time
which explode and encourage fornication and adultery in the spiritual
realm.
They try to damage us by falsely creating images of pornography and
incite desires for extra-marital sex and marital group sex.
They paint scenes of orgies and project intimate unasked for and
undesired homosexual and lesbian sexual acts as gratifying, fascinating
and as an intimacy which is to be desired and accepted as natural.
They devalue the natural desire for sex and promote habitual masturbation
as an acceptable pleasurable private or public behavior.

Devil, you and your demons' hostilities on the thoughts, dreams and imaginations of those who sleep with Christ are so disgraceful and unwarranted.

You cannot win! Not even in our sleep! Not even in our dreams! Get out and take your illusions and falsehood with you!

We know the battle is the Lord's and He will crush your head.

We know that we have the victory in the blood of Jesus because the Spirit of Truth has clothed our minds with garments of heavenly visions and positive earthly thoughts.

We command, in the Name of Jesus, that your evil strongholds in our flesh and mind be destroyed and that your demons flee from their encirclements and desist from their assaults on our dreams. Your aggression will be met with godly force and become powerless and useless in the Name and Blood of Jesus Christ.

We thank God that we can use His Word from the Bible and that we can be led by His Holy Spirit to remind these agents of hell that the eternal fire is awaiting them and that our Redeemer had already defeated the Devil's tirades in the garden of Gethsemane
and on the cross at Calvary.

That's why we love the Lord with all our mind and with all of our soul.

He is our only source of mental soundness. You cannot take away the righteousness of God in us even during periods when you think we are vulnerable, when we're at rest or in deep sleep.

Be gone lustful thoughts and dreams! Don't you know our body and our mind is the temple of the Holy Spirit? Jesus forgave our sinful mind and He transformed it.

So your battle to pull our mind into un-wholesome desires and worship of the created things and beings of this world is futile.

Storm our thoughts, imaginations and dreams as often as you may, your negativity is impotent for we have already won the victory. We worship the Creator and we will not bow to the devil's demand to conform to his need for sexual idolization and his demons' need for sexual gratification with God's chosen people. Jesus freed our minds and we are free in deed and in sleep. In Jesus Name, Amen.

Only His Blood

Your blood, Your blood, Your blood Lord is the key to my salvation.
Your blood is the only blood that protects me and cleanses me from
the evils of the world.
Lord Jesus, I praise You and I thank You for making the highest
sacrifice and for taking away all our sins and for making a way for us
to be redeemed, to be united with You and our Father.
O, Holy Spirit, deliver us from Satan through the blood of Jesus.
Cover my head with the helmet of Jesus' blood. Cover my chest with
the breastplate of Jesus' blood. Cover my waist with the girdle of Jesus'
blood. Cover my feet with the sandals of Jesus' blood.
Cover my arms with the shield of Jesus' blood and cover my body
with the garments of Jesus' blood.
O, Holy Spirit, let the blood of Jesus be poured into our hearts and
minds like His commandments and promises. O, mighty God, Lord
Jesus,
Your blood has made us more than conquerors. Your blood is the true
blood of mercy and justice and it is Your blood that gives us new life
and brings goodness into all of us.
And, it is Your blood that will shape us into a holy family, a holy
community, a holy City, a holy State, a holy Nation and a holy World.
Lord Jesus, Your blood is the key to the wisdom of the ages. It has
been Your blood
from the foundation of times which was spilled on earth to defeat hate
in order to release love and forgiveness.
Your blood is the Alpha and Omega of all life and we rejoice in the
blood of Your salvation.
Lord, Your Word promises that You will return in Your robes dripping
in blood to destroy the wicked and unjust nations of the world. And,
Your Word declares that your blood and the testimonies of the saints
are the pathways to the kingdom of God.
Lord Jesus, it is only Your blood, when we pray, that will soak up our
cares, stress and worries and then rain healing oil upon us and give us
the breakthrough to enjoy the blessings of the new covenant.
I thank God that He provided only His blood as a ransom and not
any other person or animal blood as the source of our liberation from

sin and death and as the only means of our earthly communion and eternal reunion.

Thank You, God, for sending Him to pay the price for us with His blood.

In Jesus Name, Amen.

He Regulates My Income Flow

The Lord is my Provider I will not have need of anything
even in time of difficulties because He gives me my daily
bread and He gives me the power to become wealthy.

My God never forsakes me nor allows me to beg for finances
But He makes it possible for me to prosper in all things and to
be in good health.

He plants me like a tree by the river of waters so that I can bring
forth financial fruits on every occasion of need with extra to pay
tithes and to give an offering.

My God releases wealth and riches into my life continuously and
He adds no sorrow with it. And, I can now plan to leave an
inheritance to my children and my children's children.

He has given me life abundantly and I have become a blessing to
many. He has forgiven all my debts and He has made my sleep
sweet. My God has made it possible for me to spend my days
in prosperity and my years in pleasure.

I praise my Lord everyday for pouring out such a great financial
blessing to me in my generation. But, there is not enough room
in my account to save all His wealth and that's why He guides me
to share His prosperity and to send His money on missions to the
lost, the needy, the hungry and the oppressed.

My Lord has told me not to worry about food, clothing, shelter or
even about my life because He said, it is He, Who, regulates my
income and it is He, Who, arranges for my finances to overflow.
I thank the Lord for being my treasurer, financial planner,
business partner, investor, banker, pay master and exchequer.

My Lord knows best how to manage and to distribute for He is
the source of my supply. All the gold and silver and all the

substance of the earth and the fullness on it, inside it, above it and around it belongs to Him.

So, I love and trust my Lord for giving me sufficiency always in all things. He allows money to circulate freely in my life and He causes extra to be available all the time. Thank You, Lord, for allowing an endless flow of income into my life.
In Jesus Name, Amen.

Trevor C. Belmosa

I'm So Glad

I'm so glad You found me
I'm so glad You saved me
I'm so glad You made my eyes
to see
What a wonderful life with Jesus
can be.
I'm grateful without a doubt
I'm shouting Your Name- East,
West, North, and South
Because the power of Your touch
Is like heavenly cushions on a couch.
I'm so glad You always remain the
same, You are no temporary flame
I'm so glad You will never leave me
alone, You are my sweetness and my
honeycomb
I'm so glad You are called Love
You are truly God's gift from above.
I'm so glad. I'm so glad. Being with
You I'm never sad. O, I'm so glad.
Thank You, Lord.

The Marriage Is Sealed

Thank You Father, Holy Spirit, Lord Jesus for Your love,
kindness, mercy and grace.

I bow and humble myself before Your throne and I praise
Your Holy Name. I exalt You among the nations of the earth.

Because, in the midst of rumors of another World War,
terrorism, economic hardship, political dishonesty, rising
prices, high unemployment, homelessness, deadly diseases,
earthquakes, hurricanes, drought, famine, forest fires,
huge ravishing ocean waves, global warming, nuclear threats,
space colonization, youthful rebelliousness, drug trade and gang
warfare.

I thank You, Father, for keeping me safe under Your angelic
Wings, for giving me refuge in Your spiritual sanctuary and
for keeping me protected in Your holy mansion.

I thank You that Your 'Word' in the Bible and Your Holy
Spirit gives me a peace of mind, an understanding heart and
a spirit to love despite the decaying symbols, perishing values and
vanishing monuments of the world.

When I witness these disasters and devastation and the traumas
they cause in our lives globally, I am thankful that You are
there for me to repent of my failings and inadequacies. And, I
pray that others will repent likewise.

But, Jesus, You are my hero, my idol, my guiding star. I adore
You. I love You and I glorify Your name. Lord, You are the
Sunshine in my life. You are the brightness which keeps me
from falling into the darkness of evil.

You give me reason to live, to smile and to be joyous.
You are the Soul of my soul. You are the Spirit of my

spirit and the Temple of my body. Let us be one. Let,
the marriage be sealed! Let our marriage be written down
in the Book of Life in heaven. Praise the Lord, I'm approved!
He sealed the marriage! It is written! Come, Let all rejoice
before the altar of God.

Lord, Yes I do, I truly love You with all my heart, mind, soul
and strength. I thank You for sealing me with Your Holy Spirit.
Now, let me invite all those who believe and all those who will
attend this glorious marriage ceremony. Thank You,
for making me one with You. I am overjoyed beyond
comprehension. He actually sealed the marriage!
And, we shared the Bread and the Wine.
What an amazing love! What an anointing! What a blessing!
Oh, God, Thank You, Thank You! It's Finished!
In Jesus Name, Amen.

Notes

ABOUT THE AUTHOR

Trevor C. Belmosa resides in Orlando, Florida where he is the Pastor of the Glorious Church of Christ. He holds a B.Sc., and M.A. Degree. Trevor is the author of two previous books which were self published in his country of birth, Trinidad and Tobago, the Caribbean. The titles of those books are: **The Soul of Pan** and **Freedom and Love.** The materials for this recent book, **Called By The Spirit For Such A Time As Now,** were from his recorded notes and prayers as well as from his social, military, educational, economic, political, and spiritual experiences. He is grateful to God for allowing him to share **this book** with you at this time and he prays that it will bless your life.